Gunpowder & Greasepaint

Brian Cuthbertson

The Nova Scotia International Tattoo

Co-published by The Nova Scotia International Tattoo Society and Nimbus Publishing Limited

National Library of Canada Cataloguing in Publication
Cuthbertson, Brian, 1936-
Gunpowder and grease paint : the Nova Scotia International Tattoo / Brian Cuthbertson.
ISBN 1-55109-454-1
1. Nova Scotia International Tattoo. I. Nova Scotia International Tattoo Society II. Title.

GT4013.C88 2003 791.6 C2003-903031-8

We acknowledge the financial support of the Government of Canada through the Book Publishing Industry Development Program (BPIDP) and the Canada Council for our publishing activities.

Nimbus Publishing Limited
PO Box 9166, Halifax, Nova Scotia B3K 5M8
(902) 455-4286

The Nova Scotia International Tattoo Society
1586 Queen Street, Halifax, Nova Scotia B3J 2J1
(902) 420-1114
www.nstattoo.ca

Printed and bound in Canada

Visual Research and Graphic Design:
Arthur Carter, Paragon Design Group

Illustration Sources:
Art Gallery of Nova Scotia, pages 6-7;
Dalhousie University Libraries, Special Collections, Killam Memorial Library: page 4;
Maritime Command Museum: pages 3 (bottom), 20 (top), 28 (top), 31, 34, 37, 41 (bottom right) and 48 (logo);
Nova Scotia Archives and Records Management: pages 3 (top left), 28 (bottom right), 29 (bottom left);
Halifax Regional Libraries: page 2;
Aubrey Jackman: page 8;
Private collections: pages 3 (top right & bottom), and 5.

All other images are from the Nova Scotia International Tattoo Society collection (see appendix for lists of photographers and designers).

Cover photo: In his teens, Roderick Redden performed in the tattoos of the 1980s as a re-enactor in the 84th Regiment of Foot, Royal Highland Emigrants—Nova Scotia's oldest living history organization.

Title page: The Nova Scotia International Tattoo massed pipes and drums

Contents

Foreword
How It All Began

Ian Fraser
Producer/Director, The Nova Scotia International Tattoo

When Vice Admiral Andy Collier, the commander of Maritime Command, invited me to his office but didn't ask me to sit down, I knew I had a problem. He was not happy and he got to the point very quickly: "What the hell did you say to Dr. Gordon Archibald yesterday?"

As the colonel in charge of the admiral's Army staff in Atlantic Canada, Admiral Collier had asked me to drop in to visit Dr. Archibald, the chairman of the 1979 International Gathering of the Clans, officially scheduled to be opened in July—which was less than six months away. Dr. Archibald wanted to have a tattoo as the opening of the International Gathering of the Clans, which was to be attended by HM Queen Elizabeth The Queen Mother.

"I told him he was crazy," I replied, noting with some interest that the admiral was not amused. "I advised him the sort of thing he had in mind couldn't be put together in less than a year and two years would be better."

Admiral Collier's eyes narrowed a little. "Did you tell him that if you were in his position, you'd seriously consider jumping out of his office window?"

His office was on an upper floor of the Maritime Centre, one of the tallest buildings in Halifax.

"I might have," I replied. Dr. Archibald and the admiral had obviously discussed the meeting. In fact, the admiral had it just about word for word.

"Guess what," the admiral said, pointing his finger at me. "There's going to be a tattoo to open the International Gathering of the Clans, you're going to do it and it had better be the best show this city has ever seen."

That pretty much sums up how the first Nova Scotia Tattoo was set in motion.

It happened on time (albeit without a dress rehearsal). The Queen Mother and Dr. Archibald loved it, Charlie Reynolds, the public relations manager of the Halifax Metro Centre and the Halifax media publicly gave it the quality stamp the admiral wanted, and everyone was happy.

A great deal has happened since that memorable meeting in the admiral's office twenty-five years ago. Dr. Archibald and I became friends and remained so until his death many years later. The Nova Scotia Tattoo became The Nova Scotia International Tattoo, and over the years has grown into a major international event that is now being copied all over the world. Thanks to the close relationship between the province of Nova Scotia and the Canadian Forces, led by Canada's Navy, the tattoo is a unique example to everyone in Canada of how the military and civilian communities can do something together. It has become a major tourist attraction in Nova Scotia, entertaining thousands of visitors every year. It stimulates Canadian patriotism, strengthens national unity, and, at the same time, reminds Canadians of the incredible contribution to our society made by the young men and women who have gone to war or kept the peace since 1867.

But The Nova Scotia International Tattoo would not exist without the support of thousands of Canadian civilians, members of the Canadian Forces, and participants from twenty countries who have taken part in the show or helped behind the scenes since that first, and memorable, production in 1979. They are the ones who gave The Nova Scotia International Tattoo the special vitality that no other show in this country has ever had. And they are the ones who deserve the credit for what The Nova Scotia International Tattoo has become. This is a book for them.

1.50

Introduction
On with the Show

VAdm J.A. Fulton, CMM, CD, RCN (Ret'd)
Commander Maritime Command 1981–1983

It is a great honour to be asked to introduce this book celebrating the twenty-fifth anniversary of the Nova Scotia International Tattoo. The province of Nova Scotia and Maritime Command of the Canadian Forces have been staunch backers of the Nova Scotia Tattoo throughout its twenty-five years of performances. The first Nova Scotia Tattoo was organized by Colonel Ian Fraser and Admiral A.L. Collier to honour Her late Majesty Queen Elizabeth the Queen Mother during her visit to Halifax in 1979.

My own association with the tattoo began in the following year, when I became Maritime Commander. At this time, the question arose as to whether or not Maritime Command should sponsor the 1981 Nova Scotia Tattoo. I must admit to having had some doubts, and I pondered the matter at length. If the tattoo went ahead, I anticipated a benefit in the relationship between the Navy, the city of Halifax, and the province of Nova Scotia. The tattoo would help to keep alive the history of the Armed Forces in the defence of our nation and show in a unique way that the men and women of the Armed Forces were well-trained and good citizens of Canada. I must also admit that, as an old gunnery officer, I was a patsy for the thought of guards and bands, military music, pipes and drums, naval displays, and gun runs. The decision was made to go ahead. When I saw the 1981 show, I was hooked, and I have supported the tattoo ever since.

My enthusiasm for the tattoo was felt equally by John Buchanan, then premier of Nova Scotia. Without Premier Buchanan's steadfast backing in those early days, the tattoo could not have been produced, and in those early days, the premier and I attended every performance to help guarantee a high level of morale and enthusiasm. The province's support remains essential today.

Each Maritime Commander since my retirement in 1983 has supported the tattoo, supplying an administrative staff, the pit band, marching bands, and demonstrations of skills like the gun run and the soldiers' race. This is a unique way of demonstrating pride of service and goodwill towards the community.

A benefit of the tattoo not recognized in the very early years is the warm relationship that develops with people from other countries, whose bands and outstanding entertainers take part in the show. The United States Marine Band performed in the first tattoo and appeared every year until 1995. In 1983 the Republic of Germany was invited to send a band and has continued to do so yearly since then. Many other countries have been represented by a wide range of performers: the Paris Police and the Paris Fire Brigade, dancers from Estonia, sailors from Russia, and the Flying Grandpas from Germany, to name a few. As performers from all over the world continued to appear, it became necessary in 1988 to rename our organization The Nova Scotia International Tattoo.

"Bond of Friendship," the motto of the tattoo, has been demonstrated in various ways. In 1995, when the wartime Allies were celebrating the fiftieth anniversary of their victory in Europe, the Germans were not included in those celebrations. The tattoo took a different approach: that year's show included a poignant scene with four soldiers—a German and a Canadian from World War Two and a German and a Canadian peacekeeper. Speaking with solemn conviction, the four stated: "We were once enemies but now we are friends." This act of friendship was noted later by many Germans, who greatly appreciated it.

Today the tattoo could not be mounted without the unstinting support and participation of many Nova Scotians with diverse talents; even people from beyond our provincial borders come to help in the production of our show. There are many volunteers, stagehands, costumers, lighting technicians, dancers, gymnasts, choirs, and other dedicated people on the floor and behind the scenes who give freely of their time. Over the years, the tattoo has attracted nearly 700,000 people to its doors, many of them from the United States, to see the best that Canada and other nations have to offer in military displays and other forms of entertainment.

Lastly and most importantly, it is with admiration and sincere appreciation that I thank the one man who has worked harder than anyone else to produce this show of such high quality every year since 1979: Colonel Ian S. Fraser. Through his production of the tattoo, Col. Fraser has brought together the people of many nations, creating joy and entertainment for both performers and audiences, and giving life to the motto "Bond of Friendship."

Canadian and foreign military bands and The Tattoo Choir perform in the 2001 tattoo.

1 A Tradition Unfolds

Traditions Highlights

- Origin of the Word "Tattoo"
- Beating the Tattoo in the Halifax Garrison
- Sham Battles
- Queen Victoria's Diamond Jubilee
- Aldershot and Tidworth Tattoos
- Edinburgh Tattoo
- 1958 Tattoo on Citadel Hill
- "Soldiers of the Queen" Pageant
- Canadian Tattoo and the Seattle World's Fair
- Canadian Armed Forces Centennial Tattoo

During the eighty-year struggle for Dutch independence from Spanish rule in the sixteenth and seventeenth centuries, thousands of English soldiers served in the Dutch cause. Some fifty thousand never returned. As the English armies grew larger and the sieges longer, daily military routines became necessary—among them the requirement that troops return to their town billets or their tents when campaigning, at a set time. Each evening, drummers would march through the streets recalling soldiers to their billets. The Dutch phrase *de taptoe slaan* (in Flemish *doe den tap toe*) was used to order tavern keepers to turn off the liquor taps. English soldiery serving in Holland began calling the beating of drums through streets "the taptoo." A typical soldier of fortune of his age, Sir James Turner (1615–1686), was "a 'soldier' to the backbone," but also "a learned man." In Pallas Armata's *Military Essayes of the Ancient Grecian, Roman, and Modern Art of War* (1683), he wrote of the taptoo:

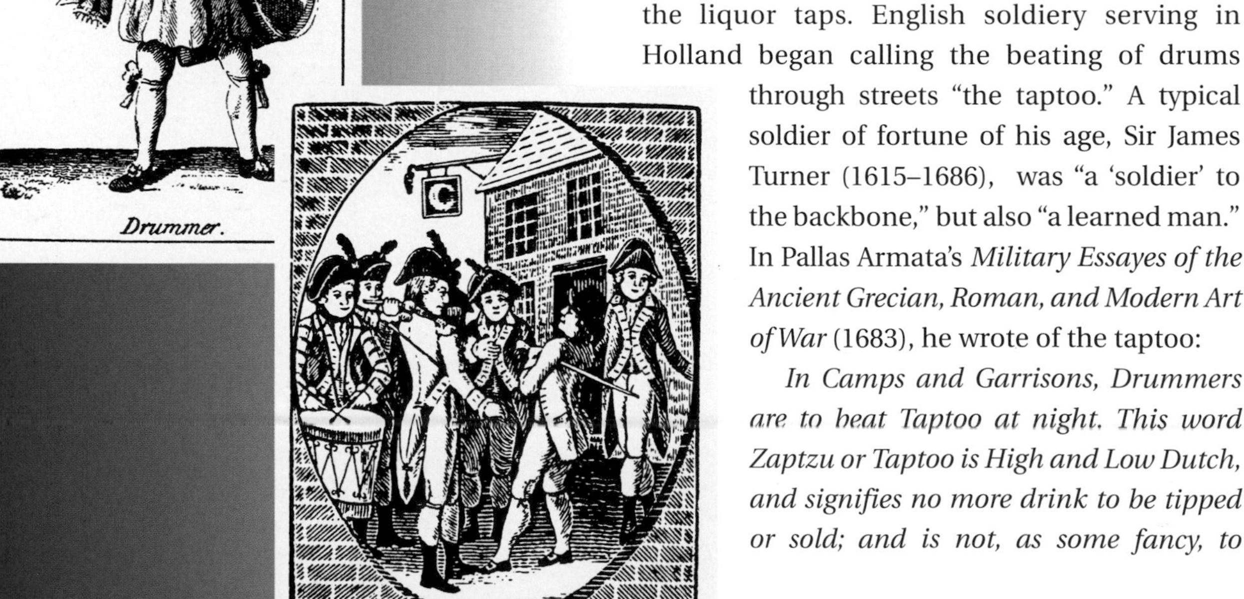

In Camps and Garrisons, Drummers are to beat Taptoo at night. This word Zaptzu or Taptoo is High and Low Dutch, and signifies no more drink to be tipped or sold; and is not, as some fancy, to advertise the Guards to place their Night Sentinels, but to acquaint Sutlers to sell no more drink, and Souldiers to go home to their Lodgings, and who is found out of their quarters after it, ought to be punished. It should beat constantly Summer and Winter, and Ten a clock at Night is the proper time for it.

Orders issued in 1644, probably for troops serving during the English Civil War, decreed: "If anyone shall bee found tiplinge or drinkinge in any Taverne, Inne or Alehouse after the hour of nyne of the clock at night, when the Tap-too beaten, he shall pay 2s 6d." During the eighteenth century, though the tattoo retained its military purpose, it became part of military reviews and ceremonial occasions. As well, over time, the spelling changed to tattoo, as in British Army Regulations and Orders of 1844: "The Tattoo is to beat at Eight o'clock in the winter, and at Nine o'clock in the summer Season."

Within the garrison at Halifax, the tattoo parade became part of the daily regimental routine. At nine thirty in the evening (in winter, an hour earlier), the evening gun was fired from the Halifax Citadel, signalling all soldiers to return to barracks. Between the evening gun and the sounding of the last post a half hour later, regimental buglers or, in the case of Highland battal-

Left: An eighteenth-century view of Halifax's St. Paul's Church and Grand Parade

Right: A triumphal procession passing by the Grand Parade —Prince of Wales visit, 1860s

Below: A painting by William Egar of the celebrations of Queen Victoria's coronation, Halifax, 1838

CANADIAN ILLUSTRATED NEWS. JULY 23, 1881. JULY 23, 1881. CANADIAN ILLUSTRATED NEWS.

NAVAL REVIEW—THE "TENEDOS" ATTACKING FORT GEORGE.

HIS EXCELLENCY AND STAFF ON THE EARTHWORKS.

VIEW FROM THE CITADEL—THE TAKING OF THE EARTHWORKS.

VIEW FROM THE EARTHWORKS LOOKING TOWARDS CITADEL.

YORK REDOUBT.

THE SHAM FIGHT AND REVIEW AT HALIFAX, N.S.

FROM SKETCHES BY JAS. WESTON, A.R.C.A.

ions, pipers and drummers performed on the parade square the time-honoured ceremony of beating tattoo. In some regiments a hymn was sung as part of the tattoo parade, "Abide with Me" being the favourite; the ceremony usually consisted of three lively tunes with intervals in between, the last one swinging into "God Save the Queen." This nightly ceremony could be heard over much of the city.

Once back inside the Citadel, soldiers formed up in their respective companies for "tattoo roll-call." Company orderly sergeants read out the name of each man. When there was no reply, the soldier was reported absent without leave. The names of those absent were reported to the guard commander, who was responsible for going in search of them. At ten o'clock the last post sounded, formally ending the military day. "Lights out" followed fifteen minutes later.

The tattoo ceremony also became part of grand public spectacles involving marching bands and military tournaments staged by the Halifax garrison. For Queen Victoria's Diamond Jubilee in 1897, with Governor General Lord Aberdeen as guest of honour, the garrison staged a splendid military tournament in the Exhibition Building. Beginning with an opening march by the band of the Royal Berkshire Regiment, the tournament followed with bayonet exercises, gymnastics, cutlass drill, acrobatics, gun shifting, and club swinging. As a finale, a sham war was staged in which British infantry came under fire unexpectedly—by a force of Afghans, no less, who retreated to a realistic fort constructed at the

Opposite: These sketches, which appeared in the *Canadian Illustrated News* in July 1881, depict sham fights and naval demonstrations. Like Halifax's early tattoos, sham fights were part of public displays put on by the military.

Military tournaments like the ones captured in these early twentieth-century photographs were also part of the grand public spectacles staged by the military.

MIMIC ATTACK ON THE CITADEL.
BOMBARDMENT OF HALIFAX HARBOR.

NO TRESPASSING

PRESTON DELEGATION

TORONTO LITHOGRAPHING CO

Previous page: Tattoos were very much a part of military and naval spectacles in nineteenth-century Halifax, a tradition continued by The Nova Scotia Tattoo.

Programme covers and advertisements for tattoos at Tidworth and Aldershot in the 1930s, and, below, The Aldershot Tattoo in 1933

north end of the building. After engineers and naval crewmen built a bridge across a river, the infantry, firing a fusillade, advanced on the fort. The engineers blew up the fort's gates, and the Afghans were taken prisoner. Performances were held each day for a week, with as many as three thousand attending a showing.

On the great Jubilee holiday of June 22, a military review on the Halifax Commons was watched by twenty-five thousand. Well before sunset, spectators crowded onto Citadel Hill and around a large square roped off on the North Common for the much-anticipated tattoo ceremony. After a display of rockets, bugles blew tattoo at nine-thirty. As soon as the music died away, soldiers lighted hundreds of Chinese lanterns and marched and countermarched to music. After the band played "God Save the Queen," a "wonderfully arranged representation of Her Majesty's face, surrounded with all colours of pretty lights, could be seen in the sky." A spontaneous roar "left no doubt of the loyalty of Halifax."

Although never as spectacular as the Queen's Diamond Jubilee, military reviews and tournaments continued to be staged by the Halifax garrison. Summertime tourists from the New England states would escape the heat of their cities and travel in comparative comfort by steamship to Yarmouth, then by rail to Halifax, while the Intercolonial Railway brought visitors from Quebec and Ontario. In the tourism literature of the day, Halifax was portrayed as The Garrison City:

What with reviews, march outs, sham battles, bombardments, parades to garrison chapel and such like, the Tommies and Jack Tars make things interesting for Halifax people and their guests during the summer months.

After World War One, with a much reduced garrison in Halifax and more soldiers living in married quarters, both the nightly ceremony in barracks and the tattoo as a public spectacle had largely ceased. However, at Aldershot, Britain's largest military station, the tattoo took on a new and expanded form, incorporating massed bands and military displays designed as entertainment. During the inter-war years, the Aldershot Tattoo, along with a tattoo at Tidworth, became highly popular annual events. At their peak as many as five to six thousand troops were involved, with massed marching bands parading one thousand men. The money raised from these tattoos went to service charities. After World War Two, another tattoo, the Edinburgh Festival, came into being. Although a festival of music and drama, it incorporated military displays and military-style bands. The result was a tattoo modelled after those at Aldershot. The first Edinburgh tattoo took place in 1950 on the Esplanade of Edinburgh Castle. The Pipes and Drums of the 1st Canadian Highland Battalion (which later became the Black Watch), then stationed in Germany, performed at the 1952 Edinburgh Tattoo.

> "...one of the most colourful and ambitious military spectacles in the history of Canada."

Inspired, perhaps, by the Aldershot and Edinburgh tattoos, in 1958 a pipe band tattoo was held on the Halifax garrison grounds and Citadel Hill to celebrate the bicentenary of representative government in Nova Scotia. The 1958 tattoo marked a revival of the ceremonial tattoo, although it was staged almost entirely by civilian pipe bands from across the province. For a moving finale, after the massed pipe bands had played "The Barren Rocks of Aden," the spotlight focused on the Citadel's ramparts and on Pipe Major Wallace Roy as the "Lone Piper" playing the slow march "The Highland Cradle Song."

At the time of its performance in June 1959, the pageant "Soldiers of the Queen," described as "one of the most colourful and ambitious military

The cast from 3 Signal Squadron for "Soldiers of the Queen," Fredericton 1959

Edinburgh Tattoo rehearsal, 1964

Seattle World's Fair, 1962

THE
CANADIAN
TATTOO
10-15 SEPT.
MEMORIAL STADIUM
SEATTLE WORLD'S FAIR
EVENINGS 8-10 P.M.
FREE TO FAIRGOERS

Poster for the Seattle tattoo designed by Captain Douglas Bell, Princess Patricia's Canadian Light Infantry

spectacles in the history of Canada," proved to be the formative ancestor of The Nova Scotia International Tattoo. Its genesis arose from the inspiration of Brigadier Robert Moncel, then commander of the 3rd Canadian Infantry Brigade at Camp Gagetown, near Fredericton, New Brunswick. A great believer in the "ennobling vision of tradition," Moncel combined traditional tattoo with pageant-style military history.

Not more than three thousand yards from Fredericton's Beaverbrook arena lay the site of an ancient French fort, which Joseph Robineau de Villebon erected in 1692, and named Fort St. Joseph. Four years later, with the French garrison greatly outnumbered, Villebon successfully withstood a siege by the New Englanders. Men of the Royal Canadian Engineers constructed a replica of the four-bastioned, wooden, palisaded fort in the arena. For script preparation, Moncel turned to two men: a young lieutenant, Ian Fraser, of the 2nd Battalion, The Black Watch (RHR) of Canada, who had been writing dramas for CBC Radio, and Captain Ian Firstbrook of the 2nd Battalion.

On the opening night, among the dignitaries attending were Lord Beaverbrook and New Brunswick's lieutenant-governor, Leonard O'Brien. Winston Churchill, no doubt at the behest of Lord Beaverbrook, was expected to attend, but in the end was unable to do so. After an animated staging of Villebon's successful defence, the 1st Battalion, the Royal 22nd Regiment from Quebec City, performed the "Beating Retreat" ceremony. The Pipes and

Drums of the 1st and 2nd Black Watch Battalions and the Regimental Band of the Black Watch gave the pageant its Scottish theme, which would remain a characteristic feature of the tattoo. Other displays included the Highland piping and dancing. Illumination in the arena consisted of a single spotlight, operated by the manager of the nearby Camp Gagetown movie theatre. Proceeds from the production went to IODE charities.

There would be no encore of "Soldiers of the Queen"; however, in 1962 Ian Fraser and a group of others with experience in staging military public spectacles created the Canadian Tattoo for the Seattle World's Fair. It proved to be an outstanding success and the highlight of the fair, despite a near-disaster that almost saw it cancelled altogether. A few days before the tattoo's first performance, a moat that circled the football field for a water-ski show was drained onto the field. The day of the dress rehearsal, a torrential rain combined with the water from the moat turned the performing field into a quagmire. At the same time, heavy winds blew down a portion of the set. Repairing the set damage was a problem, but the state of the football field was a bigger worry. A Royal Canadian Engineer officer suggested the only possible solution: pave the field. Ian Fraser marched into the fair president's office, threatened to cancel the tattoo, and demanded that the field be paved. It was paved within twenty-four hours. (Fraser later cheerfully admitted that, as a captain, he had no authority to even approach the president of the fair, much less threaten to pull the show.) The tattoo garnered publicity across the United States and was packed for every performance. Among those attending were legendary entertainer Maurice Chevalier and Elvis Presley, who was in Seattle making the film *Come to the Fair*. Elvis reportedly loved the show.

Two years later, planning began for the Canadian Armed Forces tattoo, which would be part of the 1967 centennial celebrations. Ian Fraser was selected to write, produce, and direct the centennial tattoo. What he and Ian Firstbrook created was a twelve-scene show portraying the history of Canada's Armed Forces from 1665 to 1967. One thousand and ninety-seven soldiers, sailors, and airmen would participate in a spectacle unlike any other in the world. It involved acquiring thirty-two hundred costumes, World War One Lee Enfield rifles from Australia, one hundred ancient "Brown Bess" muskets, and an equal number of French flintlocks. The show, with its total cast of seventeen hundred, travelled on two special trains and performed at forty-eight locations across the nation; it still holds the title of being the largest touring show in the world.

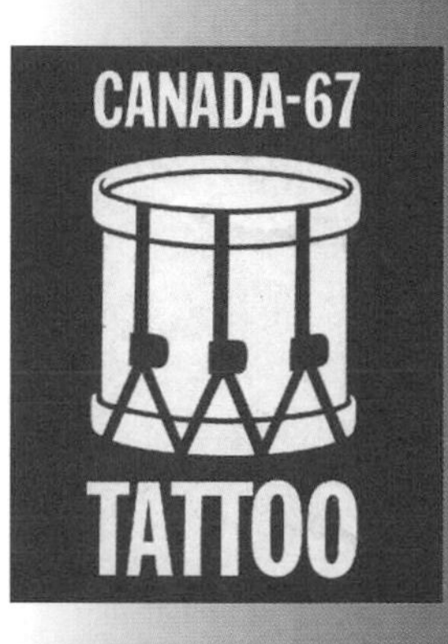

The drum logo for Canada's 1967 (centennial) Canadian Armed Forces Tattoo

The 1967 Canadian Armed Forces Tattoo finale

Canada's 1967 centennial symbol—the stylized maple leaf

The cover of the promotional brochure advertising the 1967 Canadian Armed Forces Tattoo

Performers during the 1967 Canadian Armed Forces Tattoo

2 The Tradition Takes Hold in Nova Scotia

1979 Tattoo Highlights

- The First Nova Scotia Tattoo
- Celebrating Nova Scotia's Scottish Heritage
- Creating Music for the Tattoo
- "Designing Excellence"
- Canada-Nova Scotia Concept
- A Lighting Legacy
- Tradition Through Sound
- Ian Fraser, Producer and Director
- Commentary from Above
- Tattoo Guests of Honour
- A Royal Spectacle

Canada's practice of staging ad hoc tattoos, as special occasions demanded, might well have continued, if not for Nova Scotia becoming host to the second International Gathering of the Clans. The first gathering had been held in Edinburgh in 1977, when it was agreed that the second would be in New Scotland.

The Scottish Societies Association of Nova Scotia was created to organize the gathering, but little had been done to ensure its success until Gordon Archibald agreed to lead the organization. Known as "the ultimate Tory Gentleman," Archibald was chairman of the Maritime Telegraph and Telephone Company Board of Directors and he brought to his task the top-level management expertise that had been lacking. His Scottish and Nova Scotian roots ran deep indeed; Archibald proved a master at cajoling governments, business colleagues, and not least the Canadian Forces into throwing their support behind making the gathering a success. A tattoo celebrating Nova Scotia's Scottish heritage seemed an ideal way to elevate the event, especially as Her Majesty Queen Elizabeth, the Queen Mother would be the guest of honour.

To produce the tattoo, Gordon Archibald secured the secondment of Ian Fraser, now a full colonel, who had finished his tour of duty as commander of the Canadian Airborne Regiment. For help, Fraser turned to former tattoo colleagues, many of whom had been members of the Black Watch: Major George Tibbetts, with whom Fraser had grown up in New Glasgow, became production manager; Captain Frank Grant, formerly a sergeant major in the Black Watch, took on the task of militia liaison officer; later, Don Reekie, who had been a regimental sergeant major of the Black Watch, would join the team as an assistant director. Costumes and props in Ottawa from the centennial tattoo were rescued just as they were about to be sent to the dump. Two forty-foot vans brought them to Halifax; some of the costumes are still in use today, thirty-six years later.

Unlike the "Soldiers of the Queen" pageant, which relied upon five hundred regular soldiers, the 1979 tattoo and those following it would rely increasingly on civilian performers and the militia, especially the two battalions of the Nova Scotia Highlanders, Canada's largest Highland regiment. Two Nova Scotian Highland militia regiments were formed in the 1860s and 1870s, and local pipers began to appear on their muster

International Gathering of the Clans
1979
Nova Scotia

The massed pipes and drums including cadets, The Toronto Scottish Regiment Pipes and Drums, and The Fraser Holmes Memorial Ladies Pipe Band

A Tribute to History

Nova Scotia's Scottish Heritage

Nova Scotia's Scottish heritage dates back to 1621, the year Sir William Alexander of Menstrie convinced his sovereign, King James I, that Scots emigrating to the new world should have a New Scotland as the English had New England and the French, New France. A Stuart, James ruled as James VI in Scotland. He ordered the Scottish Privy Council to prepare a grant making Sir William proprietor of the territory within the bounds of the three Atlantic Provinces and the Gaspé Peninsula—to be called for all time New Scotland, or, in Latin—the language in which the charter was drafted—Nova Scotia. Although Sir William's attempts to establish permanent settlements of Scots had to be abandoned when France regained possession of Acadia in 1632, the name Nova Scotia endured. In successive wars it changed hands numerous times, until the Treaty of Utrecht in 1713, when Britain gained permanent possession.

During the seventeenth and eighteenth centuries, many Scots crossed the Atlantic, but few came to Nova Scotia until "a rage of emigration" took hold in the Highlands in the aftermath of the failed cause of Bonnie Prince Charlie and his defeat at the Battle of Culloden. The arrival of the ship *Hector* on September 15, 1773, in Pictou Harbour, carrying nearly two hundred Highland emigrants, began a tide of Scottish emigration that would not cease until the middle of the nineteenth century. By then, Scots and their culture predominated in Pictou and Antigonish counties and throughout the Cape Breton Highlands, where Gaelic would be spoken by some as a first language into the twentieth century. Because it was so concentrated, Scottish heritage could be preserved to an extraordinary degree. It was around this heritage that the 1979 tattoo would take shape.

A group of tattoo performers in ancient Scots costume

The Highland and Scottish National Dancers of Nova Scotia

rolls. The Victoria Highland Provisional Battalion of Infantry, headquartered in Baddeck, Cape Breton, was composed almost entirely of Gaelic-speaking Highlanders and included among its corps fifteen pipers. Later, it would become the Cape Breton Highlanders and the direct ancestor of the 2nd Battalion Nova Scotia Highlanders.

Today's 1st Battalion Nova Scotia Highlanders began as the 79th Colchester and Hants Highland Battalion of Infantry, which later became the Pictou Highlanders. When originally formed, these two were the only Scottish regiments in the Canadian Militia to wear the kilt. During World War One, many men and pipers from the 94th and 79th joined the famous Nova Scotian 85th Battalion, giving it its pronounced Scottish character. During the same war, the massing of pipe bands was initiated. To mark Dominion Day in 1918, five hundred pipers from British and Canadian Forces in France met for a highland gathering, that, it was said, would have gladdened the heart of Bonnie Prince Charlie himself. Highland regiments have held massed pipe and drum performances ever since.

For the 1979 tattoo, massed pipes and drums were formed from 2nd Battalion, The Royal Canadian Regiment (created from Pipes and Drums of the 1st and the 2nd battalions of the Black Watch), the 1st and 2nd Battalions of the Nova Scotia Highlanders, 33 (Halifax) Service Battalion, the Clan MacFarlane Pipe Band from St. Catharine's, Ontario, and from the Nova Scotia Pipers and Pipe Bands Association under the charge of pipe major Donald Carrigan. A Truro native, Carrigan had learned his piping as a boy and perfected it as Pipe Major of the 1st Battalion of the Black Watch. While pipe major at the Royal Military College in Kingston he was chosen as pipe major for the Gathering of the Clans production in 1979.

For the position of music coordinator, Ian Fraser obtained Commander Jack McGuire through Maritime Command. He would work year-round in close association with the production staff, re-arranging and composing music to best fit the mix of instrumentation, while integrating the pipes with the ensemble of bands, choirs, and solo voices. His approach was "not to try to write music for musicians, but to write music for the people." Thus, much of the music written for Nova Scotia's tattoos would be original, enhancing with music the emotional and nostalgic impact of each production. The Stadacona Band would become a musical mainstay for the Nova Scotia Tattoo as its pit band. McGuire would write and/or arrange all the massed music and fanfares, with the exception of the beginning overtures and entr'actes, which Sergeant Earl Fralick arranged. McGuire also scored tunes for lone pipers, bands, and choirs as well as a prelude to O'Canada, designed to fire up Canadians with patriotic pride.

Pipes and drums and military bands were the traditional elements of tattoos. However, the distinctly Nova Scotian combination of traditional tattoo elements with theatre, historical pageantry, military competitions, choirs, dance routines and other such displays would create an

The first Nova Scotia Tattoo logo, 1979

Musicians from the Band of The Royal Canadian Regiment

Costume and Set Design

Working closely with the tattoo producer, and often after conducting research, visiting museums and examining old magazines and photographs, tattoo designers create the designs for the hundreds of costumes needed for each show. Once completed, the designs are handed over to the head of wardrobe for production in the Tattoo Costume Shop. In many cases, the designs themselves—those of Robert Doyle in particular—are stand-alone works of art.

The set from "Mother Racketts," 1992

Samples of Robert Doyle's costume designs

Robert Doyle

Designing excellence

In 1979, just before the first tattoo, Producer Ian Fraser called John Neville, Artistic Director of the Neptune Theatre, to find a costume and set designer. Neville's reply was simple and to the point: "The best designer in Canada lives here in Halifax—his name is Robert Doyle."

Doyle, who had worked as a designer for a number of theatrical productions, joined the staff for the first tattoo, and, aside from a few occasions when he's been off working on other projects, he is still with the show a quarter of a century later.

A former professional dancer, Doyle designed sixteenth-century clothing for Parks Canada, was the resident designer at a number of theatres, a founder of the Costumes Studies Program at Dalhousie University and the Stage Design Program at the University of Regina, and a designer for the Opening Ceremonies of the Pan American Games. There isn't much in the field of theatrical design that he hasn't done. His tattoo costumes cover virtually the entire design spectrum: toy soldiers, marching playing cards, ball gowns, sea monsters, butterflies, cowboys, robots, space cadets, pirates, chimney sweeps, and even a huge foam rubber caricature head of a well-known politician. He's done it all with great style, or, as some say, with Doyle style.

The pearly kings and queens in costume for the "Knees Up Mother Brown" segment at the 1994 tattoo

entirely new kind of tattoo. Called the Canadian-Nova Scotia Concept, its aim was to create a glittering extravaganza with wide audience appeal. Traditionally, military tattoos were held outdoors in the evenings, the setting sun providing a blazing backdrop for the final ceremony. At Aldershot and Tidworth in England, the tattoo evolved into a large open-air spectacle. In moving indoors, dramatic theatre staging and lighting became key factors in maintaining the critical intensity of audience experience, for a performance lasting two and a half hours or more, in an enclosed amphitheatre setting.

> "the distinctly Nova Scotian combination of traditional tattoo elements with theatre, historical pageantry, military competitions, choirs, dance routines ... would create an entirely new kind of tattoo."

Although the Halifax Metro Centre floor could be used for many purposes, it was essentially a hockey rink with a floor space eighty-five feet wide and two hundred feet long. Ian Fraser gave Robert Doyle, one of Canada's most talented costume and set designers, the task of turning the Metro Centre into a giant indoor theatre with a stage to hold three hundred. Doyle designed a stage with a three-tiered set of platforms, some eighty-five feet wide by forty-five feet high. It

Don Tremaine
Commentary from above

Alumni of The Nova Scotia International Tattoo are close to divisional strength these days. Numbered among them is none other than CBC veteran Don Tremaine, who, along with Major Doug Bell, acted as tattoo commentator and host since its inception in 1979. Looking back on his time at the tattoo, Tremaine recalls:

...sitting cheek by jowl with Doug up in the catwalk for all those years explaining and introducing the various acts, laughing at the antics of The Flying Grandpas, although we'd seen their act countless times, standing at attention for the playing of the national anthems, coping with whatever glitches occurred and looking proud and happy as the pipes and drums marched off to the strains of "The Black Bear." The audience, many with tears in their eyes, awash in nostalgia and patriotism, stood and applauded till the last note was played and the lights came up.

In 2000, after a forty-two-year career in television and radio and twenty-one years with the Nova Scotia Tattoo, Tremaine retired. He reappeared for the 2002 tattoo as a citizenship judge: in a brief ceremony on the Metro Centre floor, he swore in fifteen new Canadians during the July 1 performance. This was a significant event not only for those new Canadians but for the tattoo audience as well, many of whom witnessed the ceremony for the first time and were able to reaffirm their own oath of Canadian citizenship. (The practice is expected to continue on Canada Day during future tattoo presentations.) Tremaine, a member of the Order of Canada, retired from his position as citizenship judge in the autumn of 2002.

The Tattoo Costume Shop

Creativity and Craft

A warehouse in Halifax holds thousands of costumes and accoutrements that have been designed, crafted, or simply collected since 1979. These costumes are a silent tribute to the dedication and talent of the costume designers who have worked on the tattoo over the years—Robert Doyle, Rosemarie Gwilliam, Lin Chapman, and D'Arcy Poultney.

Many of the cutters and seamstresses who put the costumes together are graduates of the Costume Studies Program at Dalhousie University. The process of creating costumes began in 1979 when Robert Doyle, who was instrumental in setting up the program at Dalhousie, recruited the tattoo costume staff from among his students. The current head of wardrobe, Marilyn McLaren, is a graduate of that program; she has worked closely with Robert Doyle both at the tattoo and in other productions, including the Pan American Games in Winnipeg in 1999.

The costume inventory includes a wide variety of historic and contemporary costumes used in the tattoo since 1979. It also includes one of the most extensive collections of Canadian military costumes and uniforms in North America, a number of which have been used in movies and television. Many of these uniforms, especially those from World War Two and later, were donated by tattoo supporters.

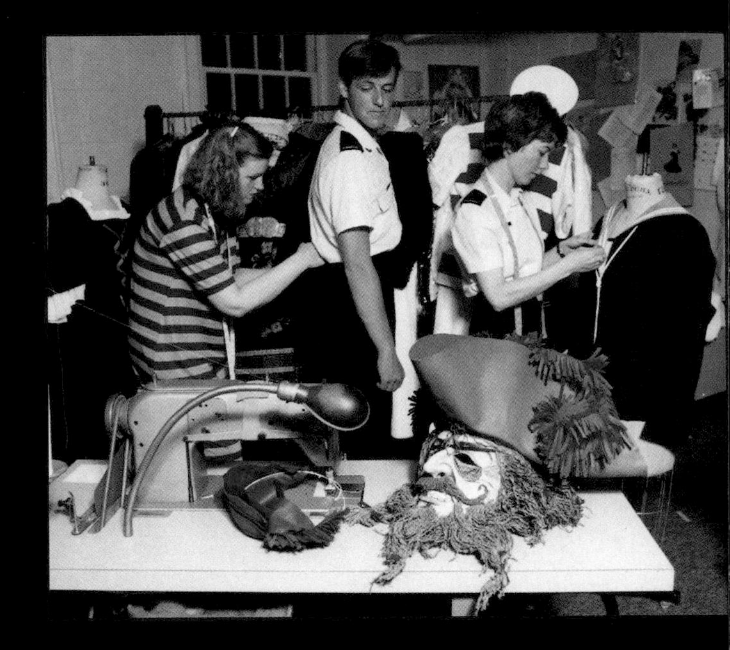

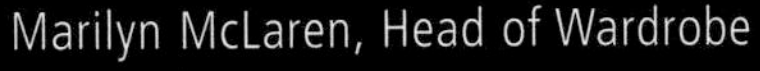

Marilyn McLaren, Head of Wardrobe

From pattern cutting and sewing to fitting, costume shop workers bring costume designs to life.

reached almost to the ceiling's catwalks and covered one full end of the rink. Strict safety measures had to be maintained. The under-supports of the initial stage were make-do affairs, but solid. The component parts were made at various work sites around the Halifax Dockyard and at Neptune Theatre workshops. The stage carpenters were all experienced carpenters from Neptune Theatre whose expertise and reputation for quality work guaranteed safety.

The sound system in the Metro Centre was primitive because the space had not been wired for anything like the tattoo before. A gerry-rigged collection of mismatched speakers supported above the stage, then covered with a motley lot of wrinkled fabric, was only a temporary solution. This proved so unsatisfactory that it had to be hurriedly re-designed before the opening night.

However brilliant the costumes, the military competitions, the massed bands, or the dramatic performances, lighting had to sharply highlight them all. It sets the mood for scenes, provides illumination, and with the use of shape and shadow, creates unusual theatrical dimensions. The task for lighting the first (and successive) tattoo performances fell on Donald Acaster, the lighting designer for over 150 theatre, dance, opera, and other spectacular productions throughout Canada and the United States. Acaster would take the production plan for each tattoo and develop a "lighting plot," which provided directions to the electrical staff on the installation of lighting equipment in the Metro Centre. Once the lights had been hung and connected by miles of cable to the dimmers and the control panel, Acaster and the console operator would programme a computer with hundreds of "cues" to follow the show from one minute to the next. During each show, Acaster cued his console operator and verbally directed the follow spot operators, telling them what colour, intensity and location he wanted at every second of the show. His mastery of lighting techniques, which he unerringly displayed year after year, gave productions an astonishing visual quality, adding to the uniqueness of the indoor tattoo.

As well as celebrating Nova Scotia's Scottish heritage in music and Highland dancing, Ian Fraser scripted for the 1979 tattoo a theatrical vignette called "New Scotland." Fraser would employ the vignette form again and again with changing themes, each designed to leave a full sensory impression through a blending of words, music, and movement. Lighting and colourful

The Calgary Police Pipes and Drums in front of the Halifax Metro Centre, home of The Nova Scotia International Tattoo

Halifax Metro Centre Galloping Horses on a tile floor!

Fred MacGillivray, CEO of the World Trade Centre Limited, which runs the Halifax Metro Centre where the tattoo is presented each year, describes the tattoo as the Calgary Stampede of Nova Scotia. He's got a point: like the stampede, the tattoo is an event that neither tourists nor locals want to miss. However, galloping horses do present a problem! Wearing small rubber boots, the horses are allowed to walk—not gallop—on the terrazzo tile floor at the Metro Centre. Along with the tattoo technical crew, Scott Ferguson, General Manager of the Metro Centre, and Ralph Williams, Event Manager, turn the hockey arena into a giant theatre for ten days every summer. They also have to satisfy the demands of the tattoo production staff, keep the giant facility running, keep the audience happy, and deal with a hundred problems a day. The tattoo holds few surprises for Williams and his staff, who have been involved in just about every theatrical venture you can imagine. From rock and roll headliners to classical concerts, world class musicals to world hockey championships, and national curling championships to political conventions—you name it, it's probably been at the Metro Centre. In some respects, handling the sixty thousand or so spectators who see the tattoo every year is barely a challenge. The tattoo is the longest running event in the history of the Metro Centre, and the staff of the arena are very much part of the tattoo team. And if there ever is a requirement for galloping horses in the tattoo, Ralph Williams and his staff will figure out how to make it happen.

Piping in Nova Scotia
Tradition through sound

As nowhere else in Canada, traditional piping has survived in Nova Scotia. Before the *Hector* landed in 1773, it is recorded that: "In honour of the occasion the young men arrayed themselves in their kilts...as she dropped anchor the piper blew his pipes to their utmost power; its thrilling sounds then first startling the echoes among the silent solitudes of our forest." With no clan chieftains to support pipers, a class of pipers best described as community pipers grew up in Nova Scotia. Gaelic speaking, these pipers "ear-learned," sometimes without any notion of the correct fingering and grace noting. Their repertoires were dictated by community tastes. A fine example of a community piper is Angus MacDonald, or "Black Angus" (1849-1939), of Antigonish—the premier piper of the day in northeastern Nova Scotia. He played for weddings, funerals, ceilidhs, picnics, step dancers and often led processions.

The Scots College Pipes and Drums of Sydney, Australia

Left: The tattoo's massed pipes and drums

Right: The Fraser Holmes Memorial Ladies Pipe Band of New Glasgow, Nova Scotia

Below: The massed pipes and drums—International Gathering of the Clans, 1991

Right: A piper from Scotch College, Perth, Australia

Pipes and drums rehearse on the Halifax Commons, 1979.

Top right: At the 1979 tattoo, "The Men of the Deeps" coal miners' choir from Cape Breton

Members of the Antigonish Gaelic Choir rehearsing for the 1979 Nova Scotia Tattoo

Programme cover for the 1979 International Gathering of the Clans

costuming accentuated these lively theatrical displays, often with a surprising unpredictability in their presentation. To this was added Nova Scotia's best-known radio voice as tattoo narrator—CBC Radio's Don Tremaine. He operated from the catwalk, which meant a seventy-two-step climb ten times a night. As well as narrating, Tremaine had the task of warming up the audience before each show, which he managed in his well-honed and admirable style.

Robert Doyle also undertook the challenging task of designing an array of costumes. Working with Doyle was Bonnie Deakin, as wardrobe supervisor. For each tattoo more than one thousand costumes could be demanded of this team, with the added requirement to design and make from scratch many others. This led in 1980 to the creation of a costume department. Between tattoos, Doyle would work on creating new designs. By April each year, he would begin the task of interpreting them to the cutters, who with the seamstresses would spend over three thousand hours to meet the challenges of authenticity and visual appeal. By the late 1980s, seamstresses would use over 146,000 metres of thread; by that time, some of the costume work had to be contracted out.

No tattoo would be complete without military competitions, which displayed, with all the excitement and tension of such contests, the military traits of agility, strength, and, above all, teamwork to the full. John MacNeil, a former member of the Black Watch and later Tattoo Festival Coordinator, organized the competitions for the 1979 tattoo. Soldiers from the two Nova Scotia Highland battalions squared off in three events: a jeep race with vehicles pulled through a figure-of-eight course, an obstacle course, and a tug of war.

Despite, only being able to have a one rehearsal in the Metro Centre arena and not a complete one, by opening night on June 28, 1979, all seemed ready for the entrance of the Queen Mother. However, tattoo narrator Don Tremaine

Ian Fraser

"You can hate me for five minutes..."

At a regimental reunion, a soldier told his former commanding officer, "I hated your guts, but I'd have followed you anywhere." That commanding officer was tattoo producer/director Ian Fraser. As a former officer in Canada's Black Watch, The Royal Canadian Regiment, and commander of Canada's elite Airborne Regiment, this was a welcome compliment—in fact, one of the best compliments Ian claims ever to have received.

During his 2001 acceptance speech when Acadia University made him an Honorary Doctor of Civil Laws, Ian received one of the few recorded standing ovations in the university's convocation history. This seems to be the trend wherever Ian Fraser is involved. It is no surprise that he has been the brain, heart, and guiding hand of The Nova Scotia International Tattoo for the last twenty-five years, blending military discipline with artistic creativity in a uniquely Canadian event.

Nothing short of genius, he has transformed the single-day event of 1979 into the culturally significant, economically important, and critically acclaimed ten-day show of today. All of this with little interest in recognition. Like an orchestra conductor, he directs participants in his affable manner, but brooks no nonsense. He's the boss. But it never feels that way as he urges all performers to do their very best—for their own satisfaction as well as that of the audience. As he puts it, "This is anything but a one-man show."

Producer, director, historian, and soldier by trade, Ian is also a brilliant storyteller. It is through his recollections, observations, expressions, and memories that we get a taste of the wisdom within. And in true Ian style, he is quick to credit Confucius, poet Alden Nowlan (who also happened to be a very close friend), Napoleon, old soldiers, his family, or his exceptional production team for a lot of that wisdom.

In what has become one of his trademark phrases at tattoo production meetings, "you can hate me for five minutes..." (a variation on an entry in Alden Nowlan's notebook), Ian readily sympathizes with the tremendous intensity and pressure show business has on its performers. "But," he adds, "get over it...the show must go on."

After twenty-five years, well over seven hundred thousand spectators, tens of thousands of performers from twenty countries, tens of millions in economic impact annually and considerable attention for Nova Scotia, it's hard to hate him (at least for the entire five minutes). As Harry Bruce once said "to create his grand spectacles, Ian can be cocky, funny, irksome, irreverent, pushy, sly, smart and bloody-minded, often at the same time. But he gets the job done."

With his passion for the arts, and his commitment to the Canadian Forces, Ian can be found reciting poetry one minute and parachuting from a plane the next. It is this wonderful dichotomy of his personality—he is a Renaissance man and a soldier both—that is so captivating. Ian Fraser leaves you thinking. And if that were not enough, his sharp wit can be quick to stun. Because, says Harry Bruce, "as every damn good soldier knows, nothing beats a surprise attack."

Ian Fraser in production meetings at the Metro Centre

The Stadacona Band

The Tattoo "pit band"

In the days of vaudeville, the pit band was the backbone of the show. In New York or London, only the very best musicians are selected to play in the pit band for West End or Broadway musicals, and no one but the most competent sits in the pit for an opera. That is why the Navy's Stadacona Band, which sits high on the bandstand at the south end of the Metro Centre during the tattoo, is known as the pit band by the tattoo production staff. As far as they are concerned, that title is the ultimate theatrical/musical compliment.

With the exception of one year when they were with the Canadian Forces in Europe, the Stadacona Band has been the pit band for the tattoo every year since 1979. The thirty-five musicians under the direction of Lieutenant Commander Gaetan Bouchard do test arrangements for Jack McGuire, Principal Director of Music, during the planning period before the show. Then they head into the Metro Centre a few days before everyone else. When the tattoo opens, the band performs the overture and the entr'acte, and background music when there are no bands on the floor. Unbeknownst to the audience, they frequently leave their position on the bandstand, dash backstage and march on with the massed bands. Then they return to provide the music for yet another scene. They also respond to those inevitable last-minute musical requirements: a drum roll or a bugle call, a rendition of a silent film piano accompaniment, backup for a soloist, eight bars of something here or thirty-two bars there, frantic script changes, or even a total rewrite with virtually no warning—it all happens.

"In the pit," with the Stadacona Band, 1990

Stad jazz from the floor of the Metro Centre

was running late. A young reporter from a local radio station suddenly found himself being briefed by Ian Fraser to stand in when, with two minutes to go, Don Tremaine appeared to the relief of all, (but none more so than the reporter).

Pipers played the Royal Salute for the arrival of Her Majesty Queen Elizabeth The Queen Mother as the guest of honour for the official opening of the Second International Gathering of the Clans. The programme began with an overture, "A Hundred Thousand Welcomes," arranged by Sergeant Fralick and played by the Stadacona Band. The tattoo continued through seventeen separate scenes: the New Scotland pageant, massed pipes and drums, bands, the Gaelic Choir, The Men of the Deeps, regimental tournaments, sword dancing, and a fantasy sequence that took a light-hearted, futuristic look at Scotland in 3001. The lack of rehearsal time resulted in a few glitches—at one point half the pipes and drums were playing one tune, while the other half played another, but no one seemed to notice, such was the enthusiasm of the moment. The finale brought forth the whole cast of five hundred military personnel and civilians to the applause of thousands of spectators, as they marched off to "Black Bear," that great Highland tune of victory. As The Queen Mother left, all present broke into "Farewell to Nova Scotia."

> "Nova Scotians had become too passionately attached to what had become their Tattoo for it to disappear."

Charles Reynolds, the dynamic and able publicity ambassador for the Metro Centre, who had in the past produced some outstanding shows for the CBC, summed up his enthusiastic feelings in saying of the 1979 tattoo that "it was the greatest show ever produced in the Centre; we may never again see one that great."

Right on the first count, Reynolds proved wrong on the second. Nova Scotians would become too passionately attached to what would become their tattoo for it to disappear. Moreover, for the Canadian Forces, the tattoo brought military and civilian circles together in a collaborative effort, and in a moving demonstration of national pride and patriotism. For the Nova Scotia government, the appeal of the tattoo as a permanent annual tourist attraction was obvious. As a show of support, the province put up the Province of Nova Scotia Highlanders Challenge Trophy, first won by the 1st Battalion, the Nova Scotia Highlanders. But what best summed up the spirit engendered by the tattoo of 1979 was when at the first performance the Queen Mother recalled the words of Dame Flora, one of the greatest clan chieftains: "The Clan family is beyond, and outside, and above divisions between nations, countries, and continents."

David Hignell
A lighting legacy

Not long before he died, Don Acaster, the tattoo's lighting designer since 1979, was asked what sort of legacy he would like to leave behind. "I've done it already," he said, "I've trained David." He did indeed, and the first person to agree would be David Hignell.

In taking over from Acaster, Hignell has put his personal stamp on lighting the tattoo. Each autumn, working from the University of Lethbridge in Alberta where he is employed as coordinator of Technical Theatre Services, he reviews the instrument list for the forthcoming tattoo. Hignell designs the lighting plot and waits for the production script to arrive in the spring. Aided by videos sent by performing groups, he plans his basic design. When in Halifax, he and his team take two days to install the massive lighting rig. At that point, his work has just begun.

When rehearsals are underway, Hignell and his technical crew face the task of programming the computer to operate the hundreds of lights, many of which contain as many as five hundred colours. The team works every night when the cast leaves—setting light levels, selecting patterns, creating special lighting effects, and choosing colours. From a box above the arena, Hignell directs the follow spots that complement the computer-generated lights. When it all comes together, the effect is amazing.

When asked what his objective is, David Hignell's reply is simple, "I'm there to make the performers look better." This modest comment is exactly what Don Acaster would have said.

Tattoo Guests of Honour
From Politicians to Royalty

Traditionally, each year the tattoo is opened by the patron of the Nova Scotia International Tattoo, the lieutenant-governor of Nova Scotia. Two governors general—Madame Jeanne Sauvé and Ramon Hnatyshyn—have formally opened the Nova Scotia Tattoo. On very special occasions, the tattoo has been opened by a member of the royal family—Her Majesty Queen Elizabeth The Queen Mother in 1979, Prince Andrew in 1985, Prince Edward in 1987, and Princess Anne in 1991.

The tattoo guest list always includes members of the diplomatic community, federal and provincial cabinet ministers, senior officers of the Canadian Forces and the RCMP, as well as a wide range of distinguished Canadians and special civilian and military visitors to Nova Scotia from Canada and other nations.

Presentation of Colours to Maritime Command by Her Majesty Queen Elizabeth The Queen Mother, on the Garrison grounds, 1979

A. Gordon Archibald, chairman of the 1979 International Gathering of the Clans, escorts Her Majesty Queen Elizabeth The Queen Mother at the Halifax Metro Centre for the first Nova Scotia Tattoo.

Her Majesty Queen Elizabeth The Queen Mother officially opens the first Nova Scotia Tattoo in 1979.

Her Majesty Queen Elizabeth The Queen Mother with Premier and Mrs. John Buchanan

HRH Prince Edward and Colonel Ian Fraser backstage

Vice-Admiral J.A. Fulton, HRH Princess Anne, Ian and Gladys Fraser and Colonel Bruce Gilchrist backstage

HRH Prince Andrew with members of the Royal Canadian Mounted Police

Premier John Savage being presented with "Tattoo Sailor" by Maritime Commander Vice-Admiral Peter Cairns

Their Excellencies Governor General and Mrs. Ray Hnatyshyn with Chief Warrant Officer Robert Farmer, Director, Quantico Band of the United States Marine Corps

The Navy

In 1980, when the Canadian Navy was seeking a vehicle to stimulate public interest in the seventieth anniversary of the Royal Canadian Navy, Vice Admiral Jock Allen, Commander of Maritime Command, concluded that the way to do it was via the Nova Scotia Tattoo. The first tattoo had been presented the year before and the Canadian Navy ran that event by way of supporting the First International Gathering of the Clans, which was opened by Her Majesty Queen Elizabeth The Queen Mother. Premier John Buchanan responded positively to Admiral Allen's request, and the province of Nova Scotia joined with the Navy to produce the 1980 tattoo. The partnership has continued ever since.

Over the years, the Navy has provided the administrative support and staff coordination for Canadian Forces participants. They also provide bands, naval displays, and cadets, and sponsor the Canadian Naval Gun Run Championship—a main feature of the tattoo for many years—drill contingents, and historic uniforms. Above all, the spirit of cooperation established many years ago has continued and has been a significant factor in making the relationship between the Canadian Forces and the province of Nova Scotia the strongest in Canada.

In 1995, when the tattoo society was formed, the Navy participated, and the mandate of supporting the Canadian Forces established by the province of Nova Scotia was strengthened. Changes have been made in the structure and the degree of participation but the Canadian Navy remains firmly committed to their show. The partnership established between the Canadian Navy and the province of Nova Scotia stands as an example to all Canadians how the people of a province and the sailors of Canada's Navy can work together to present a world-class event.

Stadacona Band musicians PO Julie Cuming and PO Don Driver on the 1995 tattoo poster

Gun Run teams lined up at the finish of a race

The National Band of the Naval Reserve

3 Growing the Tattoo

Early 1980s Highlights

In the immediate years after the successful 1979 tattoo, the practice of marrying traditional military public spectacles with theatrical staging in an amphitheatre setting continued, but became more adventurous, colourful, even magical.

It assembled pipes and drums, adult and children's choirs, and gymnasts as the mainstays for each production. Three military bands—The Stadacona Band of Maritime Forces Atlantic, The National Band of the Naval Reserve, and the Land Force Atlantic Area Army Band—started what would become a tradition as musical anchors for tattoo after tattoo. On the artistic side, a team had come into being headed by Ian Fraser as producer/director, Jack McGuire as musical composer and arranger, Joe Wallin for dance, Piper Major Don Carrigan, Lynne Pascoe Maybee and her gymnasts, Robert Doyle as costume director, and Don Acaster as lighting director. This team consistently demonstrated a combination of creativity and professionalism that brought national and international recognition to the tattoo. In a press interview, Major Aubrey Jackman, an experienced tattoo producer and production consultant to the Nova Scotia Tattoo since 1981, remarked "I would say Ian Fraser is among the three really professional tattoo producers in the world." The Nova Scotia Tattoo was the largest in North America, according to Jackman; it was modern "entertainment on a vast scale, with something to move the heart and bring a tear to the eye."

The 1979 tattoo programme had included traditional Highland dancing numbers, which the Queen Mother had greatly admired. She told Ian Fraser "those lovely young dancers…remind me of wisps of thistledown." In successive tattoos, Joe Wallin's choreography became more thematically varied and venturesome. His versatility as a choreographer was demonstrated in the 1980 tattoo, for which he created two vibrant dance scenes. The first captured the colour and movement of the hornpipe, a dance that originated in English folk traditions of the sixteenth century, but had been adopted by sailors in the age of Horatio Nelson. Wallin's choreography incorporated such movements and gestures as seamen would have used in their daily duties—shading the eyes while on lookout, or pulling on halyards to raise sail. This had to be done for five historical periods, from the War of 1812 to the post World War Two Navy, while retaining the natural spontaneity of the traditional hornpipe dance and

The Fanfare Trumpeters' costumes were designed by Robert Doyle for the 1981 tattoo.

Major Aubrey Jackman, MBE Destined for the Tattoo

In 1965, a fortune-teller in London predicted that Aubrey Jackman would have a connection to Canada. At that moment, in an officer's mess in India, a British officer was recommending Jackman as a tattoo consultant to Ian Fraser.

In 1967, Jackman joined the Canadian Forces tattoo production team and became a consultant to the Nova Scotia Tattoo in 1981.

After war service as an artillery officer, he worked in the professional theatre in London before joining his family's hotel business in Bath. As a major in the British Territorial Army, Jackman produced many military shows in the United Kingdom, including the Bath and Cardiff tattoos, the Wembley Band Show, and tattoos in Hong Kong, Belgium, and Oman.

He was awarded an MBE (Member of the Order of the British Empire) for his work on behalf of the British Army in the United Kingdom, and is producer emeritus of the International Association of Tattoo Organizers.

music. Equally demanding was the choreography for the second sequence of dances, which recognized the four principal immigrant groups to Nova Scotia. The set began with the waltz and quadrille of the Lunenburg Germans, who had settled on Nova Scotia's South Shore in 1753. That of the Scottish heritage followed, as embodied in the smooth and graceful dances of the Lowlands, then the bright and lively movements of Highland dancing in the strathspey and reel sequences. English country dancing by young dancers costumed in the dress of the mid-1700s was followed by Acadian dancers performing one of their lively and animated traditional dances. Over the years, Joe Wallin trained both an adult and a young dance company to perform in virtually every tattoo since 1979.

For the 1981 tattoo, Nova Scotians had their first view of the twenty-four fanfare trumpeters, in dress of the Tudor period. Robert Doyle designed the trumpeters' "official uniform" which, using Nova Scotian armorial emblems and the province's coat of arms, dates back to those of Sir William Alexander and the Nova Scotia charter of 1621.

With the creation in 1983 of the Tattoo Choir, under the direction of Dr. Walter Kemp of Dalhousie University, tattoo programmes gained

A scene from "The Oak Island Treasure," 1980

a new musical and theatrical dimension. The choir was composed of 150 volunteer singers, drawn from a wide variety of metropolitan Halifax choral groups: The Dalhousie Chorale, The Aeolian Singers, church choirs, the Nova Scotia Gilbert and Sullivan society, choirs of the Nova Scotian Black community, and the Dartmouth Choral Society. Initially, both adults and children sang in the same choir, but enthusiasm and success saw the establishment of separate adult and children's choirs. While Walter Kemp conducted the choir on stage, his wife Valda directed from behind the scenes, making sure everyone was in place and ready to file on stage with military precision. Over the years the choir would make a tremendous contribution to the tattoos, with members performing as soloists, quartets, small choral groups, actors, dramatic voices, and, on many occasions, extras. From its beginnings, the adult choir did not restrict its efforts to annual tattoo appearances, but sang with Symphony Nova Scotia and at ecumenical church services.

The sixty-voice children's choir, under the direction of Patricia Tupper, first appeared in the 1984 tattoo. In successive tattoos children from the choir have appeared dressed as chimney sweeps for a Mary Poppins scene, as gnomes and toadstools, and as pearls in a bed of seaweed. They give a delightful spirit and energy to the fantasy scenes, lending enchantment to each production in which they perform. All this is very demanding on the children, who range in age from nine to thirteen years. If it were not for

Civilians and the Military

Two Communities, One Show

Most tattoos presented around the world are largely military events. The Nova Scotia International Tattoo is a little different. There are, of course, military performers—the show couldn't be presented without them—but there are also a vast number of civilians involved, and the Royal Canadian Mounted Police provide support every year. This mix is what makes the Nova Scotia show different from any tattoo presented anywhere in the world. What is even more unique is the fact that the mix of performers isn't really noticed by anyone.

A cast of nearly two thousand gathers every year to present a show that really is the coming together of the military and civilian communities. They present an event that is parade, circus and theatre, with a healthy mix of athletic displays, choirs, dancers, and eclectic music. Military bands, civilian choirs, and dancers work together. Members of the Canadian Forces don unusual costumes. Germans, French, Estonians—whoever is taking part in the show from overseas that year— gets involved.

Civilians dress as soldiers and the audience wonders how a seventy-year-old choir member can still be part of the Canadian Forces.

It's a classic example of how two distinctly different cultures—the Canadian Forces and the civilian community—can come together to make history. At the same time, the standing tattoo theme, "Bond of Friendship," is alive backstage as long-lasting friendships develop between performers from around the world. A number of marriages have taken place between performers—and nothing can be more friendly than that.

A civilian choir, civilian dancers and military bands come together on the floor at the tattoo.

New naval gun carriages were constructed for Canada's Canadian Armed Forces centennial tattoo, 1967.

parents helping out each year by taking measurements for costume preparation, bookkeeping, car pooling, and chaperoning, this special contribution would be impossible.

Another new attraction involving youth was the Tattoo Gymnasts, formed in 1981 under Lynne Pascoe Maybee, a former Maritime champion gymnast and a coach for twenty years. Composed of female gymnasts ranging in age from nine to sixteen, and older male gymnasts from several gymnastic clubs throughout the province, the gymnasts perform their synchronized sequences to songs (arranged by Jack McGuire) like "Westering Home" and "Cec's Schottische."

What proved to be one of the most popular events added to the tattoo performance was The Canadian Naval Gun Run Championship, which requires the competing teams to run a challenging and dangerous course. The team that completes the race in the shortest time (with penalty seconds added on for infractions) is declared the winner and awarded the William Hall, VC Memorial Trophy, named after the first black man and the first Nova Scotian to be awarded the Victoria Cross for bravery.

In this formative period of the early eighties, each tattoo continued to be built around one or more main themes with the interweaving of supporting sub-themes. On the road to Canadian nationhood, the year 1910 marks the creation of a Canadian navy. Although at the outset it seemed to hold little promise, the Royal Canadian Navy was the third largest in the world at the end of World War Two. In the ensuing years, it participated in numerous operations in defence of Canada's maritime interests and for preserving peace. It was fitting, therefore, that the first scene of the tattoo in 1980, the seventieth anniversary of the Royal Canadian Navy's founding, should have been a tableau depicting our naval heritage. The performance took its title from that moving naval hymn, "Eternal Father Strong to Save," the first line of which is, "For those in peril on the sea." The hymn has been sung for generations by seafarers and their loved ones. Supporting scenes included "Halifax 1910," "The Hornpipe Dancers," and "A Mess Deck Medley," sung beautifully by a massed barbershop chorus. This celebratory remembrance of Canada's naval heritage was not intended as a history lesson, but rather sought to make Haligonians more conscious of the Navy's importance to their community, and to foster good relations between sailor and citizen.

Of the many thousands who enjoy the natural pleasures of the Halifax Public Gardens and admire its statuary, probably few have more than a passing knowledge of the South African War (1899–1902). The lone soldier figure in the garden's Soldier's Memorial Fountain was modelled from a photograph of a local soldier who served in the Canadian Mounted Rifles. Some seventy-three hundred Canadians fought in that war and most left from Halifax on their voyage to South Africa. The 1982 tattoo remembered these Canadians with a medley of some of the most patriotic songs ever written, none more so than Edward Elgar's "Land of Hope and Glory."

In the aftermath of the American War of Independence, an estimated thirty thousand Americans who remained loyal to Britain and the Crown came to Nova Scotia and New Brunswick as Loyalists. For the two hundredth anniversary celebration in 1983 of the Loyalists' arrival in Nova Scotia, the tattoo paid tribute to those stalwart settlers and their descendants with a special pageant and dance scene, as well as a children's fantasy scene portraying a Loyalist child's impression of this new home in a strange land.

Performers for "A Loyalist Wonderland" were drawn from Digby Sea Cadet Corps No. 26. The tattoo had begun the practice of selecting a different cadet corps within Nova Scotia each year to participate in the tattoo, especially in the fantasy scene, which by 1983 had become a permanent feature of the tattoo programme. With such magical names as "Oak Island Treasure" and "Medieval Tournament," the fantasy scenes give shows a touch of the magical, to the enjoyment of both young and old.

At the end of the 1983 tattoo, which had attracted a record thirty thousand people to performances over a five-day period, Premier John Buchanan's announcement of a further three years of funding for the tattoo came as little surprise. The tattoo's phenomenal success and economic contribution were obvious to all. It had become an internationally recognized experience of intensely visual and musical theatre, while still retaining its traditional military character. With more than one thousand performers taking part in the two-and-a-half-hour production, the Nova Scotia Tattoo had grown into a national institution without compare.

All the tasks associated with the meticulous planning of space and act sequence, down to the sergeant-major's pace stick and split-second timing, the co-ordination of lighting and movement on the floor, the scripting of numerous scenes, and the directing of performances, from the "Lone Piper" to a finale with a cast of a thousand, now required a production staff of over one hundred, some of whom worked year round. Staff worked under an almost endless list of positions: scene coordinator, seamstress, cutter, scenic painter, graphic designer, artist, property supervisor, souvenir programme coordinator, stage manager, historical advisor, sound console operator, and so on.

Over the years, the production team learned to refine the dramatic values of the tattoo. Lighting became more sophisticated; the civilian performances grew grander and more elaborate. A rear-projection screen was added so that slides of

Nova Scotia Tourism promotes the 1980 Nova Scotia Tattoo.

Second version of the tattoo logo showing naval symbols to celebrate the seventieth anniversary of the Royal Canadian Navy.

The Tattoo Choirs
Voices young and old

The first tattoo choir was organized in 1983; since then, the choir has grown from 60 to 150 voices. The adult choir is comprised of individuals as well as members of community choirs. In 1994, Walter Kemp created the children's choir, choosing performers from several city and private school choirs. Each year, they perform a number of scenes in the tattoo including the fantasy scene and the tattoo finale.

The tattoo's adult choir sings a tribute to the RCMP's 125th anniversary in 1998.

Walter Kemp
Sing along with Walter

After the Christmas carol session at the annual tattoo Christmas party, one of the guests was heard to remark, "I actually enjoyed singing tonight. That guy Kemp is amazing—he's better at sing alongs than Mitch Miller." There's a lot of truth in that sentiment. Every year at the tattoo, Tattoo Choral Director Walter Kemp makes singing fun as he gathers his choir together to produce amazing sounds.

Kemp, who holds a PhD from Oxford University, has been a member of the music department at Dalhousie University since 1977. Drawing from an encyclopedic knowledge of music, he has added Bach, Handel, Mozart, Lully, Greig, and the works of countless others to the repertoire of music performed in the tattoo. He recognizes the tattoo is musical theatre and approaches it with the same skill and enthusiasm of a Broadway choral master. Every night at the tattoo, it is easy to see that the adult and children's choirs are enjoying the show as much as he does. Mitch Miller should be so lucky.

ove: A choir
angels—
e tattoo
ildren's choir

e Standard
arers and
e adult choir
rform in a
ttoo finale.

Patricia Tupper
The joy of singing

Dressed as Mary Poppins, holding an umbrella over her head and wearing a parachute harness under her costume, Patricia Tupper flew down from the Metro Centre ceiling to her position in front of the choir and began directing fifty small chimney sweeps in a rendition of "Supercalifragilisticexpialidocious"—all in a day's work for Patricia Tupper, the director of the tattoo children's choir.

A full-time music teacher, Tupper plunged into the world of show business as an assistant choral director for the revival of "Meet The Navy" in 1980. Four years later, Tattoo Choral Director Walter Kemp "dragooned" her into organizing and directing the Tattoo Children's Chorus, which has become a fixture in the annual show.

Each year, Tupper gathers her junior choir together, recruits parents to act as chaperones, and turns those fifty young voices into an amazing musical ensemble. The children have appeared as singing pearls, farmers, and Victorian school children singing for a parade of teddy bears and various other exotic creatures. All the while, Tupper never abandons her schoolteacher persona: "Stay in line…get rid of that gum…pay attention…make sure you eat your lunch…always smile…take care of your costume…sing out…be happy…look happy…don't run backstage…"

As children's chorus director, she pulls it all together with great efficiency, good humour, and genuine affection for those she selects to be on stage. And as far as she is concerned, being suspended from the ceiling occasionally is a small price to pay for the joy of seeing her students' faces brighten when the lights come up and the applause rings out.

The Tattoo Posters
Twenty-five years and counting

The most interesting thing about the posters created every year to advertise the tattoo is that although they are displayed throughout Nova Scotia each June, they tend to vanish soon after—usually into a recreation room somewhere or to be framed and displayed by collectors around the world. If you have a poster of the 1981 tattoo created by Charlie McGuire's Theta Marketing, hold on to it—to the best of anyone's knowledge none are available anywhere. That poster, a photograph of a drummer in the Royal Canadian Regiment, is unique because of the strength of the image, but also because it was the first in a series of truly creative design work.

Pekka Kauppi, a Finnish designer living in Nova Scotia, designed the series that followed—including the striking image of a sextant set to the latitude of Halifax with rainbow colours suspended from the line of sight. David Leonard's dramatic paintings of drums and personal images stand as another example of why collectors seek tattoo posters. Then there is the work of Derek Sarty and Rand Gaynor, who took photos by George Tibbetts and turned them into dramatic posters. Ike Kennedy's painting of a Victoria Cross and falling maple leaves captured the spirit of the 2001 tattoo. Ken Webb's simple image of a World War Two sailor's cap, a soldier's steel helmet, and a fighter pilot's helmet and goggles against a Canadian flag, generated in part by computer imaging, illustrated the sacrifice of those who served in World War Two. Finally, Paragon Design Group's 2003 poster—the twenty-fifth in the series—presents a naval sword and a Scottish claymore crossed on a Canadian flag and surmounted by a silver bugle.

All of the posters tell a story. All are unique and attest to the enormously talented Atlantic Canadian designers, artists and illustrators who created them.

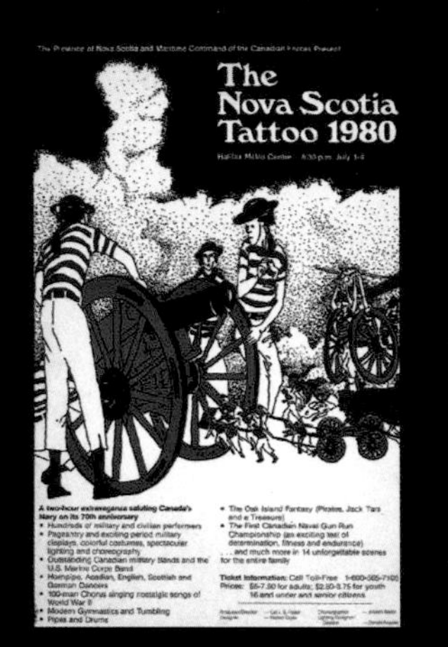

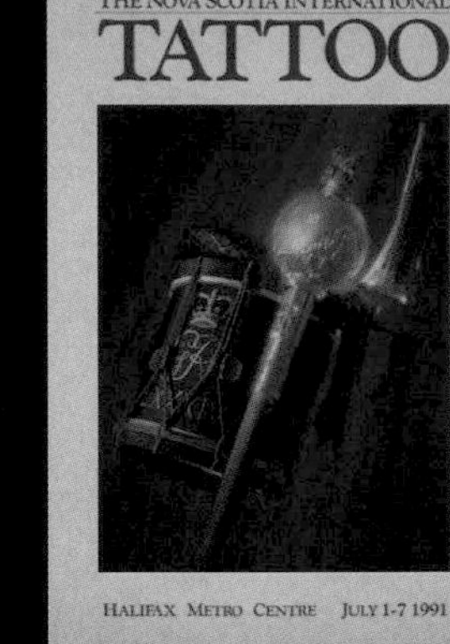

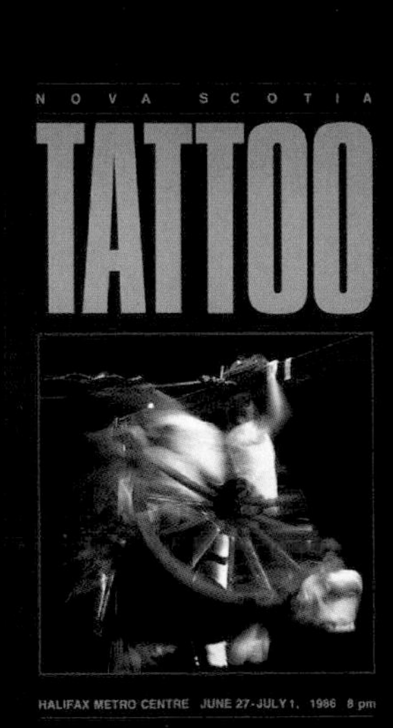

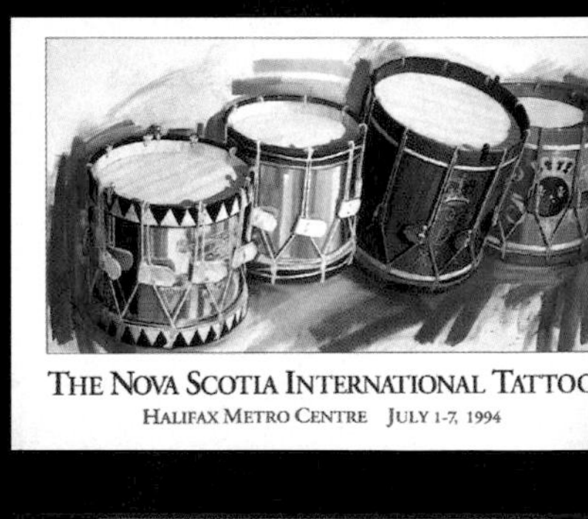

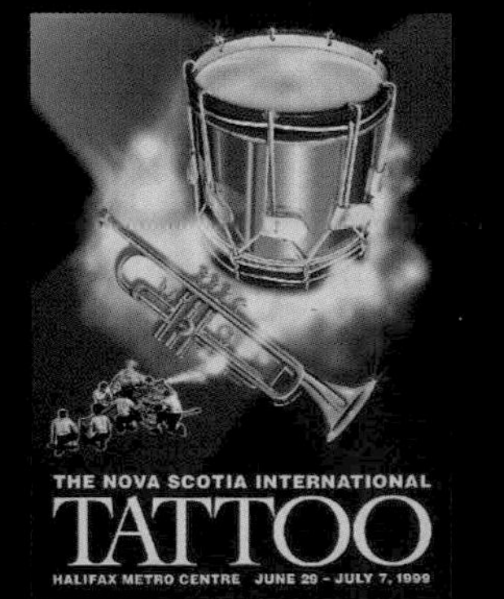

crests and various other illustrated material could be incorporated to accentuate regalia and uniforms. At the time, it was the largest rear-projection screen in the country—thirty feet high by sixty feet wide. The Pani projectors—two huge projectors with the brightest beams of light available at the time—were rented from the Montreal Opera Company at Place des Arts.

As the tattoo evolved, so too did the materials used to promote it. The design and layout of the tattoo programmes improved. Pekka Kauppi's arresting 1982 tattoo poster of a fanfare trumpeter in profile used bold and symbolic colours (red, white and blue) to advertise the tattoo, and Paul Brunelle was commissioned to design a tattoo logo. As well, the tattoo had released its first recording—musical selections from the 1981 tattoo performed by pipes and drums and military bands, from the opening overture to the finale. Proceeds from the recording went to the

The "Brunelle" logo

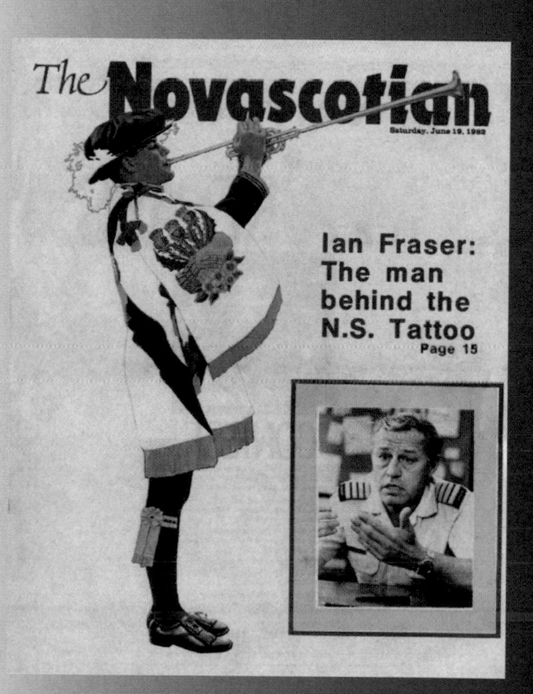

Tattoo producer/director Ian Fraser featured in *The Novascotian*, 1982

Wardroom Ball, 1910, as depicted in a Robert Doyle drawing for the 1985 tattoo

The Tattoo Dancers

Left: Dancing a salute to *The Don Messer Show*

Right: Tattoo dancers in a scene from "Brigadoon," 1991

Below: The tattoo's Highland Dancers

Joe Wallin
Step We Gaily

There's a little bit of the Don Messer television show from the 1970s in the tattoo every year. Perhaps not the Don Messer music, but there is certainly a bit of The Buchta Dancers, who were featured in Messer's show, on the Metro Centre floor every year during the tattoo.

Joe Wallin, the tattoo choreographer since 1979, was a lead dancer with that group, and the imaginative movements that helped make The Buchta Dancers famous across Canada are reflected in Joe's choreography.

A former Highland dancing champion, he has performed and taught in most major Canadian cities and has created a senior and a young dance company for the tattoo. He creates the choreography and trains as many as 150 adult and young dancers for every show. The mixture has been amazing—kick lines, dancing bears, swing numbers, jazz, minuets, gavottes, waltzes, step dancing, Scottish country dancing and always Highland dancing.

And included in all of that there is always that magic, the spirit and the fun of The Buchta Dancers that helped make *the Don Messer Show* an unforgettable television experience.

Gunter Buchta would be pleased.

Jack McGuire
Musical Innovations

"Don't worry...you'll like it!" is always the comment from Jack McGuire when he presents a new composition or arrangement for the tattoo. The interesting thing is that he is always right. McGuire has been with the tattoo every year since 1979. During those early years, he insisted on being called the music coordinator because he was too modest to accept the title "principal director of music." The fact is, there is probably no other tattoo director of music anywhere in the world with the talent of Jack McGuire.

In a career that began as a clarinet player with the HMCS Stadacona Band in 1943, he rose through the ranks, commanded the Stadacona Band along the way, and retired from the reserves in 1987 as a commander. In between, he graduated from the Royal Marines School of Music, and obtained a diploma in composing and arranging from the University of Chicago and a licentiate of music from the Royal Academy of Music in London, England.

McGuire has broken new ground, especially with his arrangements for combined bands. He skillfully integrates the pipes as an instrument in the band— an innovation he took a step further by including vocal soloists and choirs. His original works include some of the most triumphant fanfares composed anywhere in the world, and marches that will stand with Sousa, Alford, and the other great military band composers.

Put in perspective, "Don't worry, you'll like it," is really a massive understatement!

Dalhousie University Medical Research Foundation.

Employing some of the best prose ever penned about the tattoo, an unnamed newspaper reporter summed up the feelings of many when he wrote:

It always gets to me, that traditional close of a tattoo when, with massed bands and all the other performers assembled—or tightly squeezed—into the parade space, the bands play Abide with Me, followed by that marvellous and moving arrangement wherein the hymn The Day Thou Gave Us, Lord, is Ended is intermingled with the "last post." Then as the lights are doused, or dimmed, the finger of spotlight stabs through the darkness to illuminate a single piper. The sound of the last post itself, mournful yet stirring, and for me, resonant with memories, is moving enough. Followed, so it usually is at these events, by a piper's lament, it is a sequence of spectacle and sound that invariably [is] deeply affecting.

> "...the greatest show of its kind on earth"

Although in its first five years the Nova Scotia Tattoo relied almost entirely on local military and civilian performers, many of whom were volunteers, the tattoo organizers knew they had to broaden the appeal if they wanted to attract audiences year after year. They worked to attract acts from farther afield, such as the Quantico Band of the United States Marine Corps. The tattoo made contact with the United States Marines, who suggested the Quantico Band, and Jack McGuire travelled to Virginia and made the arrangements for their appearance at the Nova Scotia Tattoo in 1980. The band has marched in American presidential inaugural parades, performed before international dignitaries, and appeared in concerts, parades, and other public events throughout the mid-western and eastern United States—versatility accounts for much of the band's appeal. The Quantico Band continued to appear after 1980, invariably thrilling audiences with finely honed musicianship and parade-square precision marching.

Major Sidney Snellings, director of the Quantico Band, believed civilian acts and the use of volunteers lent variety while adding a great esprit de corps and feeling of patriotism to the tattoo. Staging the tattoo indoors meant that lighting could be used to black out departing acts while lighting up oncoming acts with no loss of pace. Snelling looked forward to coming to the tattoo each year because he had come to love Nova Scotia, its people, the freshness of the air, and the fine beer. He saw the tattoo as the "greatest show of its kind on earth," and Ian Fraser as another "Cecil DeMille." Between tattoo rehearsals, the band performed concerts in aid of the Dalhousie University Medical Research Foundation. Rarely had a good cause, wonderful music, and audience enjoyment so perfectly harmonized. The band would earn a special place in Nova Scotian hearts. On behalf of the province, Premier John Buchanan granted band members the right to

The drum corps and sousaphones of the Quantico Band of the US Marine Corps

Opposite: The band of the German Army No. 100, with Captain Reinhard Kiauka saluting VIPs

Musicians of the German Air Force (left) and Navy (below)

call themselves honourary Nova Scotians.

Europe is the homeland of tattoos and military bands. It was Frederick the Great, King of Prussia from 1740 to 1786, who first fixed the composition of military bands, thus standardizing the sound and composition of Prussian Army bands. After Germany became part of the North Atlantic Treaty Organization and underwent rearmament, thirteen major military bands were formed. In 1981 Wilhelm Jaenike, then Nova Scotia's European agent reporting to Donald Smith, provincial agent general in London, learned of the Nova Scotia Tattoo. He saw the tourism potential to the province if German and other European military bands and civilian groups

"What might be called the German-Nova Scotian Tattoo Connection had its first success."

could perform at the tattoo. He came to Halifax and met with Ian Fraser; there was a complete meeting of minds and a firm friendship formed.

The upshot was that the Luftwaffenmusikkorps 2, the German Air Force Band, performed at the 1983 tattoo. Since its formation in 1956, the sixty-member, Karlsruhe-based band had worked up a rich musical repertoire and attained an outstanding reputation through radio concerts, recordings, and appearances in Europe and the United States. The 1983 tattoo also had a theme with a German military connection to Nova Scotia: among the thirty thousand American Loyalists who came to Nova Scotia with their families were Waldeckers and Hessians, disbanded soldiers from German regiments. They settled in Annapolis County and for years local residents spoke of the "Waldeck and Hessian Lines" of settlement. Luftwaffenmusikkorps 2 caused a tremendous sensation, leaving tattoo audiences crying for more. What might be called the German-Nova Scotian tattoo connection had its first success.

The Air Force Band was followed the next year by Marinemusikkorps Ostee, the German Naval Band, which was stationed at Kiel, on the Baltic Sea coast of Germany. As a swinging dance band, the Marinemusikkorps had become much in demand all over Europe. For the 1984 tattoo, they played a special set of German band music, ending with the universally beloved "Auf Wiedersehen." In the following two tattoos, the bands of the 12th Armoured Division and that of the First Airborne Division from Stuttgart, both great crowd pleasers, would perform.

The 1985 tattoo, which celebrated the seventy-fifth anniversary of the founding of the Royal Canadian Navy, was opened by Prince Andrew, the second son of Queen Elizabeth and Prince Philip. Along with The Quantico Band of the United States Marine Corps, the American All Star Dancers from Dallas, Texas, performed. In 1986, tattoo audiences were in for something they had never seen before: the Motorcycle Display Team of the Berlin Police Force. Described as the "Ambassadors of Berlin" and the

"A Burial at Sea"—the Royal Canadian Navy's seventy-fifth anniversary commemorative tableau

Right: The White Ensign of the Royal Canadian Navy

Tattoo Volunteers and Extras

Been there, done that, got the t-shirt!

The Austin brothers, Marie Crosby, Theresa Feltmate, David and Lynne Church, Ann McLean, Lynn Blake, Jim Trainor, and Bob Wilkins (who travels from the United States) are just a few of the volunteers who join the tattoo every year to count meal vouchers, distribute posters, hand out t-shirts, and do dozens of other things to help keep the show running smoothly. Then there are the tattoo "extras," organized by David and Robin Biggs: they don costumes and appear in historic scenes carrying a spear, or dressed as a savage Scot for two or three minutes during the show. The tattoo simply couldn't be presented without them.

But there are literally hundreds of other volunteers. Every civilian performer is a volunteer, and although the military participate as part of their normal duty, many of those also give extra time to make the Nova Scotia Tattoo an exceptional Canadian event.

Volunteers in the cast and crew include representatives from just about every walk of life—businesspeople, senior citizens, teenagers, engineers, teachers, nurses, computer programmers, lawyers and doctors. Members of the provincial legislature have taken part in the tattoo and a chief of Canada's defence staff was a lone piper and an unpaid volunteer. Well…that's not entirely true. There is always a reward for those who volunteer: because of what they do in the show, everyone who attends the tattoo from this country leaves the Metro Centre every night a little prouder to be Canadian—and many of those who aren't Canadian wish they were. That's a pretty substantial reward. If that isn't enough, volunteers also get a t-shirt and a chance to go to the cast party.

Top: A dozen of the many volunteers who donate their time and talents to the tattoo

Tattoo extras dressed as World War Two personnel

The Motorcycle Display Team of the Berlin Police Force

Opposite: "The Nova Scotia Salute" at the tattoo finale in 1991

"Acrobatics in Uniform," the display team had performed around the world. Formed in 1956, it had rapidly become known for daring performances by its riders, world record holders in precision motorcycle driving and acrobatics. In September 1987, the team broke their own world record when they managed thirty-seven riders on a single moving bike over a ten-second period. They would also break their other world record by having fifty people on top of five disconnected motorcycles. Such was their ability to thrill crowds that they performed twice nightly for each show.

Attracting non-military European performers like the motorcycle team required considerable effort: Bill Jaenike, Nova Scotia's Agent General acted as the go-between in the arrangements with the team; Air Canada provided assistance to transport the team members to Canada; and Hapag-Lloyd helped with the transportation of equipment.

Beginning in 1983, members of the Canadian Forces Fleet School from the Atlantic Region formed the tattoo's Naval Display Group. In successive productions, the group executed various complex ladder displays, from wave formations to erecting a lighthouse and a precision window ladder display. Their scenes require exacting cooperation and coordination, supported by careful planning and many hours of practice. Each year a new group of these active young sailors appears, eager to participate.

In 1987, Halifax was once again host to the International Gathering of the Clans. Prince Edward, third son of Queen Elizabeth and Prince Phillip, arrived to open the games and to inaugurate the ninth Nova Scotia Tattoo. Never before were so many pipe bands participating. As well as Pipes and Drums of 2nd Battalion, The Royal Canadian Regiment and the 33rd Service Battalion, there were those of the 48th Highlanders of Canada, the Toronto Scottish Regiment, and the Lothian and Borders Police Band of Edinburgh. The Lothian and Borders pipe band is the official band of the Royal Company of Archers, the queen's bodyguard in Scotland. It has won many world championships, and has performed in Canada, the United States, throughout Europe, Russia, and Japan. After the 1987 tattoo, it played at events held during the Highland games in Halifax, Pugwash, and Antigonish.

The Air Force

Depicting the Battle of Britain, the greatest air battle of World War Two, is a little tricky in an indoor arena.

Unlike the Navy and the Army who perform displays that are based on the fundamental things they do every day, doing something similar for the Air Force can present a challenge. But on the theory there are no problems, simply challenges, the Air Force and the tattoo staff solved the problem.

The Battle of Britain was depicted by a group of Royal Canadian Air Force responding to the signal to scramble. One dashed to a replica 1940s Spitfire, the engine started, the wheel chocks were pulled away, the lights faded to darkness and the sound of an aircraft taking off traveled down the arena floor. Seconds later when the lights came up the Spitfire was gone and the ground crew "watched" it disappear. A short voice-over sequence followed and Canada's role in the Battle of Britain was told.

The same impact was achieved with a huge Sea King helicopter model that appeared from overhead with rotors moving simulating a rescue at sea.

The contribution of the Air Force did not stop there. They have provided pipe bands from as far away as Cold Lake, Alberta, regular and reserve bands from across Canada. And, of course they are always there as part of the tri-service Canadian Forces Guard that is frequently involved in the opening of the show and always front and centre in the finale. In between, they double as extras and help keep the show running smoothly.

As the staff says, depicting the Air Force in the Tattoo is not a problem—just a challenge.

Top: A replica 1940s Spitfire—one of the most famous aircraft of World War Two—commemorates the Battle of Britain at the tattoo.

The sound of the Spitfire starting up fills the arena before the lights go out

The Canadian Air Division Band from Winnipeg, Manitoba

The RCMP

The RCMP is surely the ultimate Canadian symbol. When they lead the massed bands onto the floor every night to open the tattoo, there isn't a Canadian in the audience that doesn't feel a surge of pride when they see those scarlet jackets, Stetsons, and highly polished brown riding boots. The tourists are equally thrilled. As far as they are concerned, the Mounties are really what Canada is all about.

The relationship between the tattoo and the force goes back to 1982 when Superintendent Calvin Bungay organized a contingent from the Nova Scotia Division of the RCMP to celebrate the fiftieth anniversary of the RCMP in Nova Scotia. That was a great success and, since then, the RCMP has been a regular feature in the tattoo.

Not only have they led the massed bands, they have provided police dog competitions, a ceremonial troop performing cavalry foot drill, comedy dog acts, vocal soloists, pipers and drummers, and escorts for royal visitors.

They have depicted soldiers from 1 Provost Company in World War Two and have dressed in historic uniforms celebrating their service in the North West Rebellion, the South African War, World War One and, more recently, United Nations service.

The troop that first performed cavalry drill in the tattoo now forms the core of the RCMP National Ceremonial Troop. Trained by Sergeant Major Robert Gallup and Staff Sergeant Major Debbie Reitenbach, the troop has appeared in the Edinburgh Tattoo, the Brussels Tattoo, the Netherlands National Taptoe in Breda, and is scheduled to participate in the Hamburg Police Show and the Berlin Tattoo in Germany.

Commissioner Giuliano Zaccardelli, Assistant Commissioner Dwight Bishop, Chief Superintendent Bill Vye and Inspector Keith Sherwood have made it all happen; and The Nova Scotia International Tattoo is richer for the association.

The RCMP Dismounted Cavalry Drill display

Left: RCMP flag bearers leading the massed bands

The Cadets

In 1979, a group of cadets performed as robots from outer space, captivating Her Majesty Queen Elizabeth The Queen Mother and establishing a long-standing tradition of cadet participation in the tattoo. From that first production, cadets ranging in age from thirteen to eighteen have appeared in every show.

Working with the young dancers and the junior choir, the cadets have taken part in a series of colourful fantasy scenes. From an imaginative piece involving painters' ladders to an authentic 1775 drill display from the early British Manual of Arms, they have provided a range of military and athletic displays. From the ranks of the cadets have also come extras in historic scenes, administrative and protocol staff assistants, and young musicians and pipers. In fact, there is not much the cadets have not done in the tattoo. They have added a special dimension to the show and, at the same time, have taken something away: meeting and mixing with performers from twenty countries, they have developed a much keener sense of what it means to be Canadian.

In the end, the cadets would be the first to admit the tattoo is the highlight of their year.

Sea cadets perform a rigging display at Sackville Landing as part of The Tattoo Festival

Atlantic Area Tri-Service Cadet drum major

Precision and synchronization: Tri-Service Cadets in one of many displays to entertain tattoo audiences throughout the years

4 The Tattoo Goes International

1980s & 90s Highlights

- Nova Scotia Tattoo adds International to Its Name
- Celebrating Our Ethnic Diversity
- Soldiers' Obstacle Race
- 1988 Finale
- Re-thinking the Tattoo's Corporate Structure
- Tattoo Fantasy Scenes
- "Bonds of Friendship"
- Gymnastic Display Teams
- Techies and the Backstage Crew
- Celebrating the 125th Anniversary of the RCMP
- [illegible]

By 1988, the Nova Scotia Tattoo had become a joint venture of the province of Nova Scotia and Maritime Command. At the apex of this partnership was, on the one hand, the province's premier in 1988, John Buchanan, an ardent supporter of the tattoo since its inception, and, on the other hand, vice admiral in charge of Maritime Command in 1988, C.M. Thomas. Nineteen eighty-eight, then, proved to be the watershed year for the tattoo and the organization that runs it. In recognition of how much it had evolved since 1979, and at the suggestion of Ken Mounce (then the manager of the Halifax Metro Centre), the name was formally changed to The Nova Scotia International Tattoo.

The province and Maritime Command selected a committee to run the tattoo's affairs—the forerunner of the present board of directors of The Nova Scotia International Tattoo Society, formed in 1994. A former commander of Maritime Command, Vice Admiral J.A. Fulton, who was later to chair the board of the tattoo society, chaired the Tattoo Committee, an admixture of civilians and military personnel. This committee oversaw both the production and support staffs directly responsible for creating each tattoo. Ian Fraser, retired from military service, headed the production team, which was almost entirely civilian, though many had served in the Armed Forces, especially in the Black Watch. The support staff was almost entirely military and was commanded by a colonel, primarily because it had the logistical and administrative responsibility for the over two thousand performers and backstage staff.

Lesley Preston of Mount Allison University had been responsible for building the props for each production since the first tattoo. As stage manager, Bob Burchell, with Canadian Forces personnel to assist, continued to ensure that all performers and their props were positioned on the Metro Centre floor, set, or overhead for each scene. Later, Harry Philpitt took over as back stage coordinator. He was replaced in 2002 by Mike Muldoon, a recently retired naval petty officer. The smooth running of the show depended to a large extent on the efficiency of the tattoo arena masters. CPO1 Pat Laming-Russell, who has served longer than anyone on the backstage staff, was appointed the senior arena master, and as such is responsible for coordinating movement on and off the stage, a task that can involve

Tattoo gymnasts demonstrate flexibility, strength and grace on the floor at the tattoo.

Jim Forde
"Tuba Time"

Having an absolute passion for the tuba is not necessarily strange, though it is a bit unusual. But then, so is Jim Forde. Witness the fact that he created a tuba band for the 1991 tattoo. That is a bit strange in itself. What is even more peculiar is the fact that each of the twenty-five or so tuba players was dressed in white tie and tails, and sat in small carts pulled by giant teddy bears!

A former musician (tuba of course) with the Canadian Navy and director of The Stadacona Band for five years from 1988 to 1993, Forde was also with the Canadian Forces tattoo office in Halifax for seven years prior to joining the tattoo production staff as production coordinator. After moving to the production side of the house, Forde became a member of the "Gang of Five" (the production planners).

When he is not working on the tattoo or playing the tuba with brass groups and bands in the Halifax area, he is adjudicating bands, which takes him across Canada and to the Caribbean. As if that weren't enough, he is also the manager of the National Youth Band of Canada. Given Jim's passion, the potential for talented new tuba players coming out of the youth band is great indeed.

as many as six hundred performers who have to be in position in the darkness in less than fifteen seconds.

For the 1988 tattoo, extensive changes were made to the sound system in all areas of the arena so that they could be all controlled by the sound console. Months of planning, the installation of state-of-the-art equipment, and ten miles of cable would produce the sharp sound that did much to turn the arena into a theatre. The complexity of the theatrical lighting system had grown with the show as well. Don Acaster directed sixteen spotlight operators to keep up with the movement and colour changes needed to produce the entrancing effects so enjoyed by audiences.

"...a glorious medley of melodic and harmonious songs from the repertoire of Black music."

The 1988 tattoo opened with the usual overture by the Stadacona Band and a trumpet fanfare. After musical acts with such titles as "Halifax—The Gateway to Canada" and "A Touch of Scotland" came the first stunning surprise of the show: The Flying Danish Superkids. One of Europe's most popular and impressive gymnastic groups, the Superkids consists of versatile performers ranging in age from six to twenty-four. They dance and perform expert tumbling routines as well as modern gymnastics for competitions. But it was their high-flying, amazing acrobatic gymnastics that tattoo-goers thrilled to on this group's first Canadian visit. They performed in both the first and second acts of each performance.

A major theme of the show was a celebration of Nova Scotia's ethnic diversity. Tattoo organizers had contacted the community of North Preston, the largest Black community east of Montreal, and asked them to create a choir to portray the musical ancestry of Black Nova Scotians. Out of this request came The North Preston Ancestral Community Choir, under the direction of Ernie Simmonds. Members ranging in age from thirteen to eighty were drawn from North Preston-area church and community groups. Pride of place, however, goes to The Gospel Heirs, a gospel choir composed of seven members from the Smith, Fraser, and Simmons families who had begun singing together in their North Preston church as a means of ministry through song. In a number called "The Blacks of Nova Scotia," The Gospel Heirs, accompanied by the Community Choir, sang a glorious medley of songs from the repertoire of Black music.

A keen rivalry among Nova Scotia's militia battalions has always existed. For the 1988 tattoo, Halifax's Princess Louise Fusiliers and the West Nova Scotia Regiment joined the two battalions of the Nova Scotia Highland Regiment in a competition for the Normandy Cup, in which seven-man teams from all four units were pitted against each other nightly during the tattoo. The obstacle race began with the dismantling of two machine guns. The parts and ammunition had to be carried over and under seven different obstacles, including over a balance beam, after which the weapons had to be re-assembled and fired. After the competition on the final night, the Princess Louise Fusiliers were declared the winner, having defeated the 1st Battalion Nova Scotia Highlanders, 55 seconds to 1:06 minutes.

A first for tattoo audiences in 1988 was the continuity drill display by The Queen's Colour Squadron of the Royal Air Force. The squadron, keeper of the Queen's Colour for the Royal Air Force, provided the escort when the Queen's Colour was paraded. Comprised of eighty young men, the squadron was ranked as one of the top drill units in the world. At the tattoo, it presented the drill for which it is famous: some 350 separate movements executed without a single verbal command.

If 1987 saw more pipe bands than any other tattoo, in 1988 it was the military bands that dominated. In addition to regular bands like the Stadacona Band, there were bands of the Princess Patricia Canadian Light Infantry, Canadian Forces Air Command, the Canadian Forces School of Music, the United States Marine Corps, and the 10th Armoured Division of the German Army. All told eight such bands performed a wide variety of music.

Naval participation in that year's tattoo once again saw a crowd-pleasing display by the Canadian Forces Fleet School and the Gun Run, which had lost none of its excitement. But what

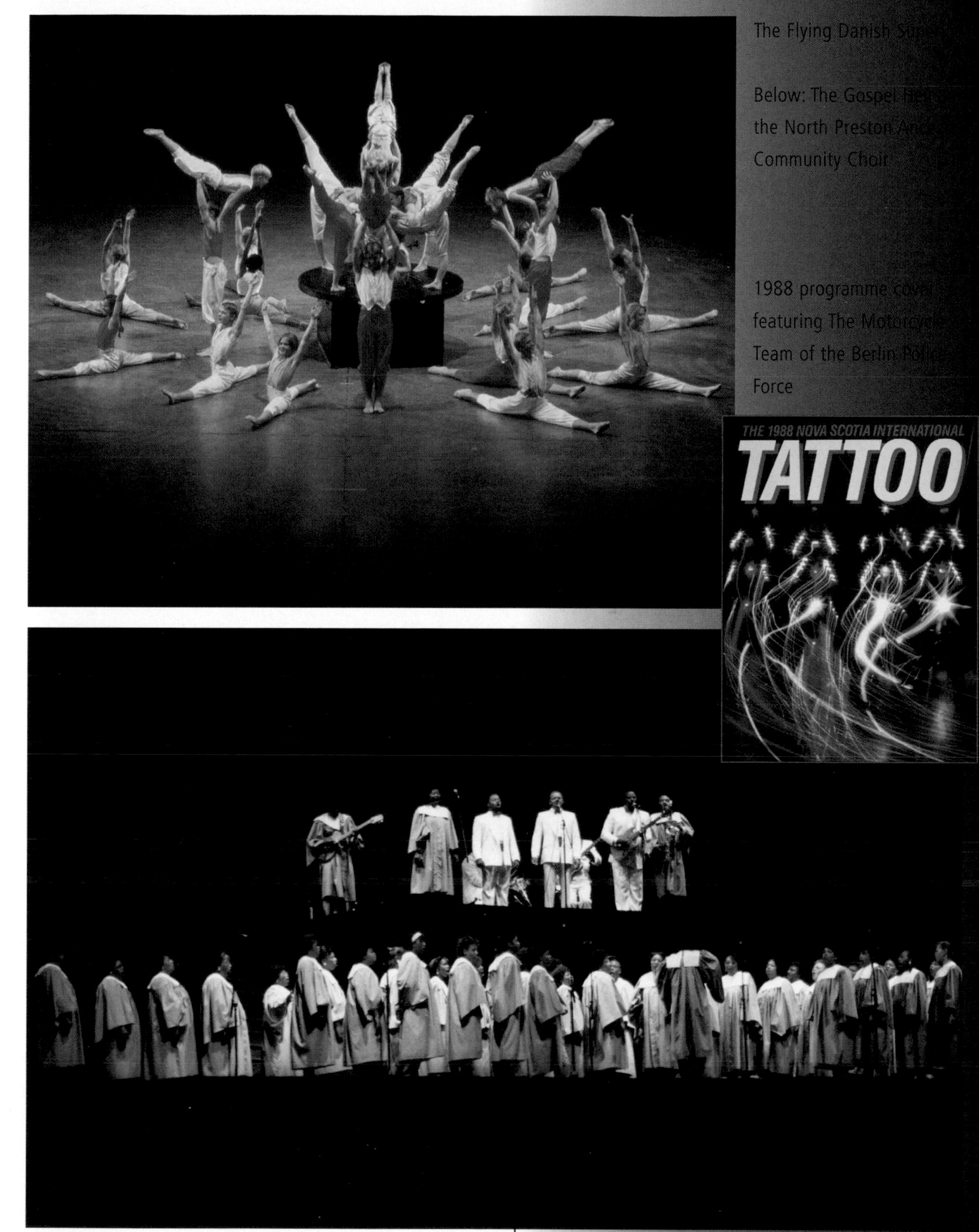

The Flying Danish Su

Below: The Gospel He the North Preston An Community Choir

1988 programme cover featuring The Motorcycle Team of the Berlin Police Force

drew the most amazement from the audience was the display of a radio-controlled model of a Sea King helicopter undertaking a rescue mission. Its designer and builder, Arie Hakkert, had created other such radio-controlled props for previous tattoos, including a flying fish, a yellow submarine and a Lancaster bomber. The helicopter had operating main rotors, which were fully speed-controlled, and a tail rotor, which could be reversed, if required, for theatrical purposes. Hakkert had crafted the model by hand from wood, foam, and fibreglass.

The 1988 finale proved to be the most magnificent and enthralling ever. It began with a fanfare to represent first post, the time of evening when the first sentries are placed around a camp. Then the armed guards—who in the past ensured order and protected the camp—were marched on to music from the massed bands. The "march on" followed as the performers paraded into the arena. The Tattoo Choir sang, unaccompanied, the traditional evening hymn, "Abide With Me," before the last post sounded. As in Highland regiments, a lone piper played to bring an end to the evening's ceremony. Before marching off, the massed bands played the national anthems of the participating counties, with the tattoo choir singing them in their native languages. On a single command, all the performers marched off the floor, until the massed and combined bands left the arena playing "The Black Bear," the Highland tune of victory. The audience broke out in tumultuous applause and a standing ovation. On the remarkable success of the 1988 tattoo, Ian Fraser commented, "It couldn't have happened anywhere but in Halifax—in Nova Scotia—because of the relationship that exists between the Canadian Forces and civilian communities."

In many ways the tattoo had become like a large corporation. It actively sought sponsorship from businesses willing to assist with specific acts: Scotsburn Dairies, for example, supported the Flying Danish Superkids in coming to Halifax; to others the tattoo sold advertisements for the programme, which had grown into an impressive publication with an enlarged format. The 1988 programme cover was one of swirling colour created by photographing the Berlin Police Display Team at a slow shutter speed. Another promotional venture, The Tattoo Festival, entertained the lunch-time crowd with concerts on the Grand Parade in central Halifax. On one occasion, passengers travelling on the Halifax Harbour ferry found themselves treated to a performance by The National Band of the Naval Reserve.

The province of Nova Scotia contributed annually to production costs for the tattoo, but both inside and outside of the government, questions were being asked about the amount of support. In response, tattoo staff demonstrated that the event injected a sizeable amount into the provincial economy; it also generated considerable sales tax revenue for the province, double the amount that the government provided

Opposite: Tattoo finale, 1996. For performers and audiences alike, the most moving part of each year's production is the finale.

"It couldn't have happened anywhere but in Halifax—in Nova Scotia..."

A militia soldier poses for a photograph prior to the obstacle race.

from the 1999 tattoo
morating the 250th anniversary
unding of Halifax

xtras as early settlers to Halifax

the tattoo. There was also the economic multiplier impact on the local economy. Halifax was so convinced of the tattoo's value that the municipal government started making a contribution to production costs.

Although staff hoped by extending the 1988 tattoo to seven days that attendance would rise to 56,000, no one anticipated the phenomenal success of such a move. Based on audiences for the main dress rehearsal and the seven public performances, the final count had surpassed the so-called "sell-out" number. The final night's performance on July 4 drew the largest single audience in the event's history.

As the 1980s drew to a close, it was decided that the 1989 tattoo would take a retrospective look at the tattoo's ten-year history. A series of historical vignettes were chosen to represent the final years of noteworthy decades in history. In "Halifax 1779," a street scene with soldiers and townsfolk was featured. Set on the Grand Parade, British troops were portrayed as travelling to and from the former thirteen colonies during the American War of Independence. The year 1809 was King George the Third's seventy-first birthday. For this scene, Royal Marines and Royal Naval seamen acted out the celebrations for the royal birthday. "The Province House 1869" scene recalled a celebrated ball held in Halifax for the visit of His Royal Highness Prince Arthur in that year. Soldiers of the Royal Military College from Kingston, Ontario, performed period drill in "The Old Eighteen 1879," while troops were entertained in their camp during "South Africa 1899." The magical creation of a little bugler's dream came next, followed by other past remembrances.

In each show, the Nova Scotia tattoo concept called for a balance between military and civilian components. How Canadian military history was being interpreted within the context of this balancing act became a matter of some public debate. On one side, there developed a feeling that the time had come to demilitarize the tattoo. It was not that the tattoo glorified war, but some felt it sanitized the idea of war, over-sentimentalizing the role of our military and over-romanticizing our history. Tattoo officials countered that the shows were anti-war and pro-military, and had as their primary aim the fostering of good relations between military and civilian communities. Conversely, in the mid-1990s, some people felt that the military segment was being diluted by too many civilian entertainment acts. Although there could be no definitive way to resolve the balancing question, the Reverend James Fraser, of Trinity-Stephen's United Church in Amherst, made some thoughtful and relevant comments after seeing the 1991 tattoo:

We were treated, too, in the harmonizing of National Pride with International Goodwill. We

Tattoo Gymnastics

Flic-flacs, whip-backs and ice packs

Monks, punks, and dwarfs swinging, flipping, spinning, and twisting. Sounds more like a Dr. Seuss tale than a gymnastic act in the tattoo, but gymnasts and acrobats from across Canada and around the world have injected sparks of athleticism, grace, and artistry into the show since the tattoo's inception.

Here is a sampling of some of the world championship teams and critically acclaimed soloists that have displayed their strength, agility, and flexibility from their various acrobatic disciplines: from Germany, The Flying Grandpas, Gym Wheel Team Taunusstein, and The Flying Saxons; from Scandinavia, The Flying Superkids, the Malmo Girls, and The Flying Stevens; from France, The Paris Police and The Paris Fire Brigade; from Switzerland, The Gymnastics Club of Mels and the D'Holmikers; from Estonia, Club Piruett; and from Canada, the tattoo gymnasts.

Using everything from parallel bars and tumbling strips to ladders and mock Viking ships, gymnastic acts frequently leave tattoo spectators out of breath. As the Tattoo Gymnasts' shirts say, "To air is human, but to flip is divine."

Centre: The Paris Police Gymnastics Team
Top right: Germany's Flying Saxons
Bottom right: Club Piruett from Estonia

The Drum Corps of HM Royal Marines

equally applauded and loved the performers, regardless of whence they came, and when, during the finale, we joined the bands and choirs in the national anthems of these countries, we were passionately part of a world united, yet knowing and feeling that our deepest devotion and gratitude were for our own nation. How much we need to repeat such experiences as these, to learn and sing the national anthems of other nations, and to feel ourselves one with others, for we all are God's children.

Although the 1989 tattoo received many accolades, attendance was down slightly from 1988, largely because tourism had been down for that year. As part of the continuing effort to evolve, tattoo staff decided to replace the then earthtone colours used in the arena with navy blue to provide a sharpened focus on the performers during necessary blackouts. Robert Doyle organized the production of a custom colour—a velour-like Prussian blue—and a matching paint was custom mixed. Curtains, rink board covers, door coverings, and matching felt coverings for the concourse walls were purchased, all in the same blue. At the suggestion of Don Reekie, an assistant director, metallic gold rink board markers were manufactured to help orient the performers on the floor. Crests consisting primarily of maple leafs and wreaths of silver and other symbols were created in large scale, then coated with heavy-duty sparkle dust to add elegance.

The tattoo had been conducting audience surveys since 1981; by the 1990s, these surveys showed that one third of the audience was comprised of tourists. Indeed, the chief justification for the provincial government's major commitment to the tattoo was the event's draw as a tourist attraction. The Department of Tourism and Culture provided funding for numerous other festivals, many of which used the tourism claim as support for their applications, but these were funded in total from a budget half that of the tattoo's funding. On this disparity, one critic of the tattoo asserted that the generosity of tattoo funding was the greatest error then being made by the Department of Tourism and Culture. When Donald Cameron succeeded John Buchanan as premier in 1991, he was determined to deal with the mounting provincial deficit. He not only ended ten years of annual increases in the tattoo's government funding, he also reduced it immediately by nearly half.

> "...the fostering of good relations between military and the civilian communities."

The tattoo had begun seeking corporate sponsorship and other means of lessening dependence on government and ticket sales before the cut was announced. In 1990, Petro-Canada came forward to sponsor the naval gun run event. As a means of creating loyalty to the tattoo, a "Friends of the Tattoo" group was organized and *The Tattoo Times* publication was created. The bi-annual newsletter was mailed out free with information on tickets, items for purchase, and behind-the-scenes articles. By the end of the decade, its mailing list would reach twenty-four thousand.

To promote ticket sales, more emphasis was placed on the tattoo festival programme, which included regular, free, noontime performances in Halifax and Dartmouth. A typical daily schedule saw the Flying Danish Superkids perform on the Grand Parade, the Light Infantry Corunna Band from Britain at the Dartmouth ferry terminal, and the Gym Wheel Team Taunusstein Show Group of the German Olympic Federation at Historic Properties. As well as performing in the tattoo festival programme, bands and other performers from the tattoo created Halifax's First of July Parade. John MacNeil took on the organizational responsibility for what would become a traditional presence by the tattoo and the Canadian Forces in these Canada Day parades, watched by as many as fifty thousand spectators.

Groups also gave performances outside of Halifax. Canada Day 1990 found the Pipes and Drums of the Queen's Gurkha Engineers playing at Kentville, the 49th Regiment (composed of cadets) at Liverpool, and the Berlin Motorcycle Display Team and the Copenhagen Police Band at Westville in Pictou County. As groups reached out beyond the bounds of Halifax, they were met by busloads from surrounding communities arriving nightly to attend performances.

The government's position on reduced funding required a major re-thinking of the tattoo's corporate structure. Becoming a not-for-profit

Don Reekie
Don't waste my time, & I won't waste yours

That is one of the first things the cast hears when Don Reekie gets to work on the finale. It takes him about an hour to organize close to two thousand performers for one of the most impressive sights in any arena in the world. With his team of former and serving members of the Canadian Forces, including Chief Warrant Officer Tom Peet, drum major of Canada's Ceremonial Guard, and John MacNeil, a former sergeant major, he polishes the image, moving performers on the floor, adjusting for visual balance, and ensuring that the colours of the uniforms and costumes work together.

Reekie, a former regimental sergeant major in The Black Watch, The Royal Canadian Regiment and the Canadian Airborne Regiment, takes it all in stride. A "charter" member of the famous "Gang of Five" that plans the show, he is involved in every facet of the production. When he is not working with the producer/director to set up the floor for the thirty or so scenes in the tattoo each year, he's troubleshooting, looking for those small problems that can become big ones.

When it all comes together, Reekie does his best to fade into the background and let others take the credit. That's fairly typical of a good former regimental sergeant major. That's also one of the reasons Don Reekie is quietly becoming a legend in the tattoo business.

Tattoo Fantasy Scenes
Chickens, Teddy Bears and Maypole Dancers

A year or so ago, a visitor from abroad commented that because children performed in the show, it wasn't really a tattoo. The remark was based on the fact that at that particular performance, fifty or so young dancers were performing as chickens...and loving every minute of it. That visitor should have been around for the past twenty years or so to see the small performers portraying toy soldiers, pearls, underwater creatures, dancing robots, circus animals, maypole dancers, teddy bears, and a wide variety of unusual animals and creatures from outer space.

It has all been done in the spirit of good fun and good entertainment. These youngsters, along with the gymnasts, have grown with the show and have become as much a part of the tattoo as the military musicians, the soldiers' race, the gun run, and the drill contingents. One of those, who joined the tattoo as a nine year old, is now an executive on the tattoo staff. Others have joined the military, and all of them have retained a warm feeling about the show in which they performed.

Strictly speaking, a tattoo is a single drummer marching through the streets, warning the innkeepers to turn off their taps. The Nova Scotia Tattoo is a performance and a celebration of tradition that, in these parts at least, includes children.

Top: A view of the maypole dancers, toy soldiers on parade and "The Chicken Drill" from the 2002 tattoo

Far left: "The Teddy Bear Picnic," 1990

Below: A group scene from "Tales of Mother Goose"

Opposite page: Gym Wheel Tea
Taunusstein, Germany

private sector society seemed the best solution. Such a move, however, required smart business planning. The tattoo would have to expand its revenue sources and be managed as a professional business with viable long-term financing. Heather Kitchen, a well-known theatrical consultant (later managing director of San Francisco's American Conservatory Theater), took on the task of preparing a five-year plan. Out of her report and the general re-thinking inspired by it came the tattoo's present mission statement:

To produce and present a world class international event that will stimulate Canadian patriotism, educate youth, recognize our country's debt to the Canadian Forces and the Royal Canadian Mounted Police, attract tourists to Nova Scotia, strengthen international relations and enhance the commercial position of tattoo sponsors.

> "...my only regret is that every single Canadian does not have the opportunity to see the tattoo."
>
> —*John Sobey*

What replaced the previous joint province of Nova Scotia and Maritime Command hierarchical structure was The Nova Scotia International Tattoo Society, officially formed in April 1994. Initially, the society consisted of the five founding members—George T.H. Cooper, Jack Keith, Ian Fraser, Vice Admiral J.A. Fulton (Ret'd), and Marilyn Atkinson—although it would grow until it averaged about seventy-five members drawn from the civilian and military communities. Its membership would expand to include all former board members and those who had made a special contribution to the tattoo. In this latter category, only Don Tremaine has been so honoured. Others members would include all former Nova Scotia premiers since 1979, as well as all previous commanders of Maritime Command. At its annual general meetings the society appointed a board of directors to formulate policy guidelines for the tattoo organization.

Also in 1994, Sobeys, the supermarket chain headquartered in Stellarton, Nova Scotia, became the major sponsor. At the time John Sobey commented: "Nova Scotia can do something no other part of Canada can...my only regret is that every single Canadian does not have the opportunity to see the tattoo. It has become the best show of its type presented anywhere in the world and is a remarkable event for Nova Scotia."

In coming forward when it did, and with a continuing commitment, Sobeys made forward planning possible. The support also came at a time when the Canadian Forces were faced with increasing overseas commitments, while the federal government cut both the defence budget and force numbers. In 1991 the demands on the Navy during the Gulf War resulted in the Gun Run being pulled for the tattoo that year, and stalwart performer for many tattoos,

Cover of *The Ta*
Times newslett
advertising the
show's twenty
year

The 1996 tattoo programme cover

Sobeys, the major sponsor of
tattoo, participates in a noon
Tattoo Festival concert by His Ma
the King's Guard's Band of
on the Halifax Grand Parade.

The Technical Crew

Techies to the Rescue...

The Russian sailor's bass baritone voice booms through the Metro Centre. But something isn't right. The orchestra is too loud for the singer. His microphone isn't working. "Scrapper" Stevenson realizes the Russian has forgotten to turn it on. He calmly walks onto the floor and hands the soloist another microphone. Precious few of the audience of six thousand realize Scrapper has even been there.

A soldier hung up on a rappelling line has no way to get down until "Mongo" (Neil Andrews) appears, coming down the rope from the ceiling and with great skill lowering the soldier to the arena floor. The audience thinks it's part of the act.

The show is in sequence rehearsal and changes have to be made. A short item is needed fast—the production team comes up with the concept, but sound tapes have to be prepared and new lights programmed. And it has to be ready in fifteen minutes. Al Strickland is given the sound problem, Robert Brassard and Brian Dawe program the lights, and it is completed with time to spare.

Repairing the audio system, getting one of the largest lighting rigs in the world up and running in twenty-four hours or so, failing microphones, stranded soldiers, and last-minute changes are all in a day's work for the tattoo technical crew. Under Technical Director Colin Richardson, the crew from the International Association of Theatrical Stage Employees (IATSE) have supported the tattoo from the first show in 1979.

Sound Engineer Alan Strickland

Crew Chief/Moving Light Operator Robert Brassard

the Band of the Royal Canadian Regiment, was disbanded in 1994. When the American Department of Defence required all military bands to be present in the United States on each fourth of July, the tattoo lost the highly popular Quantico Band of the Marine Corps, which had performed at every show from 1980 to 1996.

"...the tattoo reached out to military and civilian performers from nearly every European country and from Asia."

Since the first tattoo in 1979, coordination of Canadian Forces' support was assigned to the director of regional operations, later to be designated the chief of staff regional operations, at Maritime Command headquarters. The director, who reported directly to the commander of the Canadian Navy, was an army colonel who also assumed the appointment of tattoo commanding officer. Ian Fraser was the first, followed by David Ells and Bruce Gilchrist, the last army officer to command the tattoo.

The Canadian Forces tattoo staff had to deal with the myriads of responsibilities relating to tri-service participation in the annual tattoo. Varied tasks included liaison with military performing groups from Canada and overseas, protocol issues, provision of technical support, transport, food services, and security.

In 1992, as part of a restructuring of the Canadian Forces, Regional Operations was disbanded and the responsibility for coordinating Canadian Forces' participation in the tattoo was taken on by the Naval staff at Maritime Command headquarters. Captain (N) Arthur Vey was the first; he was followed by Commanders David Beresford-Green, Barry Munroe, John Creber, and Pat Charlton.

The participation of the Canadian Forces in the tattoo was based on a memorandum of understanding, initially between Maritime Command and the province of Nova Scotia and later between Maritime Command and the tattoo society. Over the years, the tattoo society assumed many of the responsibilities formerly undertaken by the Navy.

A small tattoo office, established by the Navy to coordinate Canadian Forces' participation in the tattoo, was staffed largely by personnel from the reserves who were employed as needed on a casual basis. Connie Matheson, who had been with the tattoo on the Canadian Forces' support side for many years, continued as secretary and office manager. She provided continuity, and to some extent became "the corporate memory bank" for Maritime Command.

Although the Navy continued to be responsible for Canadian Forces' participation in the tattoo, Maritime Command was moved to Ottawa in 1997. The Canadian Forces' tattoo coordination was then handed to Maritime Forces Atlantic in Halifax. As a result of reduced resources, the tattoo had to rely more on volunteers, particularly

Backstage
Kicking the top off the ant hill

Backstage during the tattoo has been described as looking like an anthill with the top taken off.

It is organized chaos, with upwards of two thousand performers milling about, changing into costumes, moving bits and pieces of equipment around, fastening that last button, or tying a piece of ribbon before going on stage. Making things work backstage is the job of Mike Muldoon, the backstage coordinator. Keeping everyone safe falls to tattoo safety officers Peter Beech and Chief Petty Officer Denis Descoteaux.

Then there are the unsung heroes of the tattoo: the arena masters. They are responsible for moving everyone and everything on and off the stage and the arena floor. Although the team changes year to year, the key players are always the same—Chief Petty Officer Pat Laming-Russell, a public servant and a naval reservist, Master Seaman Brian Bennett, Petty Officer Al McKenzie and school teachers Teresa King and Jake Wttewaal.

Their job appears simple...until you try it. Work in semi-darkness...Change scenes in less than five seconds...Load the set with hundreds of performers in ten seconds...Make sure everyone is on the right mark when the lights come on...Don't damage anything or anyone when moving heavy equipment in the dark...Be ready for anything. The backstage team also routinely handles stage fright, dropped instruments, performers who don't understand English, and the adrenaline that effects everyone when the curtain opens and the lights go on. They do it all with good humour and a great deal of skill. Given fifteen seconds to do something, they would probably wonder what to do with the other ten.

Arena masters—backstage organizers

Countries Participating in the Tattoo "Bonds of Friendship"

A display of participating nations' flags, 1993

Army, Navy, and Air Force cadet corps from around the province. The Royal Canadian Mounted Police had first appeared in the 1982 tattoo, when a marching contingent and a police dog display team participated. There had been return visits, but from 1994 the RCMP became a permanent presence in the tattoo in association with the Army, Navy and Air Force. Where before international groups had come from a few countries, particularly the United States and Germany, in the 1990s the tattoo reached out to military and civilian performers from nearly every European county and from Asia. Although Germany would still remain the main source of overseas performers, others would come from Australia, Belgium, Denmark, Estonia, France, Ireland, Japan, Korea, Netherlands, New Zealand, Norway, Portugal, Russia, Sweden, Switzerland, and United Kingdom.

Among the overseas military bands new to the tattoo was the Royal Netherlands Air Force Band, accompanied by a huge barrel antique organ. It took a Royal Canadian Air Force Hercules aircraft to transport the organ, 275 costumes, scenery, and props for the band's song and dance routines. The Principal Band of the French Foreign Legion, known as "Les Kepis Blancs" because of their trademark headgear, made its first North American appearance at the 1997 tattoo.

Considered among the most versatile bands in the world because of their ability to perform in orchestral, concert band, and dance combinations, as well as being a superb marching band, the Band of Her Majesty's Royal Marines appeared twice in the 1990s. A Halifax music critic paid the band a glowing tribute: "... in matter of substance and sonority they sound massive right across the tonal spectrum, downright symphonic in fact. The amount of sound this band of thirty-seven musicians produces is astonishing in its evenness and consistency."

From "down under" came the Australian Army Band—Brisbane. When The Central Band of the Japan Air Defense Force marched onto the Metro Centre floor at the 1999 tattoo, it was an historic moment as the occasion marked the first time any major Japanese military band had performed outside of Japan. All told, twenty-nine different international military bands appeared at the tattoo in the nineties. Canadian military and civilian bands also performed in greater numbers and variety than ever before. The Woods Manufacturing Company Brass Band from Ontario would perform in four tattoos. In a symbolic connection between the world's largest outdoor show, the Calgary Stampede, and the world's largest indoor show, the Nova Scotia International Tattoo, the Calgary Stampede Band joined the tattoo for its twentieth anniversary production in 1999.

No tattoo could be without massed pipes and drums, whose numbers kept growing. As well as the regular performing pipers and drummers, numerous military and civilian pipe bands would make appearances. Some, like the Fraser Holmes Memorial Ladies Pipe Band from Pictou County, were Nova Scotian. Fraser Holmes of Pictou County had organized and trained many young bands over the years. Many in the Fraser Holmes Ladies Pipe Band, first organized in 1982, were once Fraser's students. Other civilian bands came from Britain, Australia, New Zealand, and across Canada. Among these was Scotland's McNaughton Vale of Atholl Junior Pipe Band, reigning junior champions of the 1993 World Pipe Band Championships in Glasgow. The "Vale" was

> "...the first time any major Japanese military band had performed outside of Japan."

composed of forty-two of the finest eleven-to-eighteen-year-old pipers and drummers in the world. Another internationally renowned group was the Scots College Pipes and Drums of Sydney, Australia, who marked their school's centenary by coming to Nova Scotia for the 1993 tattoo.

With the exceptions of the tattoo's own gymnastic team, that of the Navy's Fleet School, and one from Australia, all other gymnastic display teams came from Europe. Of these, three proved the most popular with audiences. The Flying Grandpas gave their first performance in 1991; they would return year after year. The group is comprised of Hamburg Police officers who combined athletic ability, artistic skills, and an irrepressible urge for fun in hilarious vaulting and trampoline displays. In Germany, they were known as "Cops of First Entertainment." Tattoo audiences were also privileged to witness the

Central Band of the Japan Air Self Defence Force

ating the 125th
ersary of the Royal
dian Mounted Police,

sheer daring, split-second timing, and athletic ability of the Paris Police Gymnastic Team. During one of their acts, the tension was so high that complete silence reigned while they performed a remarkable and terrifying high-wire balancing feat. The Flying Danish Superkids continued returning to the tattoo to display their rhythmic acrobatics and classical dance routines. The single overseas military gymnastic group was that of the Royal Australian Navy Physical Training Display Team, which performed an electrifying routine of chair tricks, cutlass swinging, and vaulting displays.

New display groups performing in the 1990s ranged from the Estonian Club Piruett's rhythmic gymnastic team, world champions in aesthetic gymnastics, to the Korean International Taekwondo Mission Display Team. Club Piruett would become a favourite of audiences with their spiralling ribbons, breathtaking juggling of golden hoops and trios of young women diving simultaneously through hoops flung across the arena. From the Netherlands came the Juliana Bicycle Team, whose members constructed human pyramids while cycling. In a welcome gesture of the Cold War's end, the Song and Dance Ensemble of the Russian Northern Fleet appeared in 1993. But it was the Imps Motorcycle Club from London Dockyards that truly captivated audiences. In all, they consisted of forty boys and girls, ranging in age from six to fifteen, who performed a complex series of manoeuvres, with the youngest members riding minibikes and the oldest, full-size off-road machines. A charitable organization, the

Above: Royal Band of the Belgian Ai

Left: Principal Band of the French For
Legion

Fanfare Trumpets of the Australian Ar

Above: The Calgary Fiddlers

Right: The New Zealand pipe band, "Pipin' Hot"

Pipe Major, Queen's Gurkha Engineers

club sought out young people considered to be high-risk, and challenged them to aspire to outstanding achievements.

The 1990s proved to be a decade of major historical commemorations, beginning in 1990 with the fiftieth anniversary of the Battle of Britain, to pay tribute in Winston Churchill's immortal words, "Never in the History of human conflict has so much been owed by so many to so few." It was with these hallowed words that Don Tremaine concluded his account of the Battle of Britain for an introductory piece in the programme. For the Battle of Britain scene, Arie Hakkert created a three-quarter scale model Spitfire fighter as part of a scene that simulated an English fighter base, with scrambling pilots and life-like battle noises. In a brief ceremony at the same show, ninety-one-year-old Sydney Morgan Jones of Halifax was presented with a framed photograph of a corporal in the Royal Canadian Regiment in World War One dress. At seventeen, Jones had been among the first blacks to serve with the Canadians in France. As a member of the Royal Canadian Regiment, he saw heavy fighting in a number of battles and was wounded at Passchendale.

Princess Anne opened the 1991 tattoo in conjunction with the Fourth International Gathering of the Clans. This tattoo proved to be the largest yet, with eighteen hundred performers. More than nine hundred musicians performed in seven military bands, seven pipe bands and two choirs, including the Australian Army Band—Brisbane, the Marinemusikkorps Nordsee from

Sets and Props
Just Give Us Time...

Designed in 1979 by Robert Doyle and modified extensively over the years by other designers, including Lesley Preston and Fred Allen, the tattoo set is an unusual theatrical structure. Each year it is built in forty-eight hours or so, previously under the direction of Phil Sorge, and today, under the supervision of Set Coordinator Mary Jane MacLeod.

The multi-level stage, one of the largest indoor stages in the world, covers the entire end of the Halifax Metro Centre and incorporates a huge rear projection screen. This enormous structure, which turns the arena into a vast "theatre in the round," is designed in such a way that it can be filled with over five hundred performers in under ten seconds.

Then there are the tattoo props. The bridge of a corvette, ornate carriages, French ballet hobby horses, swords, spears, backdrops, set pieces, muskets, sea monsters, and just about anything else you can imagine has been made by the props staff.

Arie Hakkert, an uncompromising craftsman, has constructed some remarkable stage properties for the tattoo. He has built a three-quarter-scale World War Two Spitfire, a scaled Lancaster bomber, and a two-thirds scale Sea King helicopter, all radio controlled. These aeroplanes were donated by the tattoo to the Shearwater museum, where they are on permanent display. Over the years, props managers have included Lesley Preston, Jennifer Wyatt, Mary Sadoway, Sara Hollett, and Patricia Martinson, a senior citizen who builds props with the energy of a twenty year old.

The motto of the props shop says it all—"The difficult we can do immediately and the impossible just takes a little longer."

Above: Set constructed for United Nations peacekeeping theme

Top right: A scaled version of a naval Spitfire

Arie Hakkert constructing his "Sea King" helicopter

Connie Matheson

Finding solutions is a full-time job

She's never angry, never excited, and, to the best of anyone's knowledge, has never refused a request for help or advice. When it comes to the tattoo, the word "no" is simply not in her vocabulary. That attitude pretty much sums up the contribution made by Maritime Forces Atlantic's Tattoo Secretary Connie Matheson to The Nova Scotia International Tattoo.

Since 1982, Connie has been the mainstay of the tattoo's military office and is the only full-time member of the Canadian Forces tattoo staff. As a result of her vast experience with the show, she has become the Canadian Forces' tattoo corporate memory and encyclopedia—she can answer almost any question about the participation of the Canadian Forces in the show or anything for which the Canadian Navy is responsible.

Connie sums up her lengthy tattoo experience clearly: "The tattoo is good for the Canadian Forces, it's good for the community, the province, and the country and it makes me proud to know I'm a part of the tattoo team." And the tattoo team is very proud of her.

Germany, and the Atlantic Region Cadet Pipes and Drums. Ten of the numbers were especially aimed at children; in the case of "Once in the Highlands," adults were treated to such songs as "Brigadoon." This tattoo brought from a young German performer the comment that, at home, when soldiers had finished for the day, they took off their uniforms because there were "difficulties with the feelings in the community," but in Halifax he could go out in the streets in uniform and see respect. He recognized a relationship between the Canadian Forces and the civilian community, one he said he'd never seen anywhere else.

Themes for the 1993, 1994, and 1995 tattoos related to World War Two. For the 1990 tattoo programme, Don Tremaine had written about the Battle of Britain; now, for the 1993 programme, Jim Lotz prepared the first of a number of concise background histories on other themes. In 1993, it was the Battle of the Atlantic, in which Canada's fledgling Navy played a major role. In 1939, the Royal Canadian Navy consisted of 14 ships and 1,674 men; by the end of World War Two, Canada's "corvette navy" had grown to 471 fighting vessels, supported by 99,688 men and 6,500 women. Lotz's descriptive prose, the poignant musical medleys, theatrical vignettes, and Don Tremaine's narration complemented each other to give a holistic understanding to these historical events. It became a way of teaching Canadians their history—sight and sound blended with the written and spoken word.

Unquestionably, the most moving and theatrically successful thematic portrayal was that of the Normandy D-Day landings on June 6, 1944, by 15,000 Canadians on Juno Beach. One reviewer of the 1994 tattoo wrote of how "the D-Day invasion scene began with the pounding rhythm of Gustav Holst's "Mars" from the *Planets* thundering out fatality and dread, and when the guns start up, the cannonade of explosions and small-arms fire blast away at you from every corner of the compass, building to a terrifying crescendo of fury." Smoke, the roar of artillery, and the staccato bark of machine guns thundered through the Metro Centre as an eighteen-year-old Canadian soldier wrote a letter home from a ship in an English port on the night before the dawn landing. Another reviewer described the Metro Centre:

being filled with artificial smoke, anti-invasion obstacles created the impression of the Canadian land-

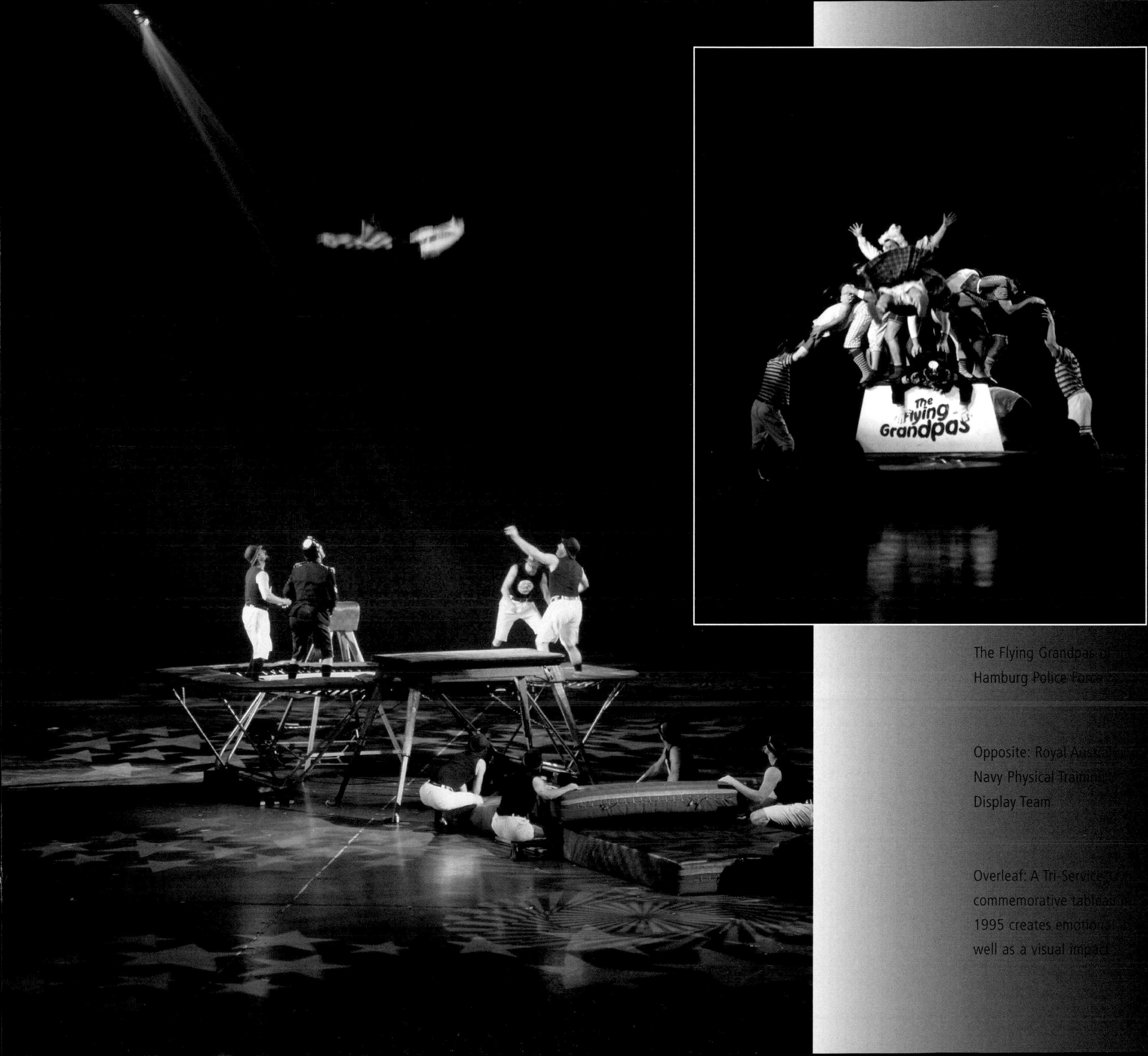

The Flying Grandpas of
Hamburg Police Force

Opposite: Royal Austral
Navy Physical Training
Display Team

Overleaf: A Tri-Service
commemorative tableau
1995 creates emotional
well as a visual impact

CWO Tom Peet
There's something about a soldier

The drum major of the Band of the Ceremonial Guard and a former regimental sergeant major of the Foot Guards, Chief Warrant Officer Tom Peet is cast from the mold of the old-fashioned army drum majors. They held the bands together and gave rise to the statement by an old soldier that a good military band is worth a thousand cannons.

An efficient drum major is the right hand of the director of music or the bandmaster, and epitomizes the highest standards of drill and discipline. He has a vast knowledge of military music and understands and respects military musicians. He also must be an outstanding soldier. Tom Peet is all of those.

Tom has a few other traits as well—he loves military music and pageantry, and is creative and flexible. He is immensely loyal to the Ceremonial Guard and The Nova Scotia International Tattoo, where he is the drum major of the military bands, an assistant director of the show, and a member of the production planning committee. He first joined the tattoo in 1991, and has been an invaluable member of the tattoo team ever since.

If Tom Peet were the drum major of that band the old soldier talked about, it wouldn't be worth a thousand cannons. It would be worth twice as many.

ing zone, Juno Beach, on the Normandy coast, while the noise of heavy artillery and small arms fire echoed throughout the building. And through the mist came files of actors dressed as young soldiers, the whole scene strongly reminding us of those fine young Canadians who landed on that beach on June 6, 1944, so many years ago. The artefacts, the simulated dead and wounded lying and sitting to one side, the soldiers piling supplies, the jeeps and Bren Gun carriers rolling through and above the band playing a medley of vintage D-Day music…Even more soul stirring was the parade of ghosts of those men who fell on D-Day, who walked slowly and silently through the "beach" after the landing.

> "It became a way of teaching Canadians their history—sight and sound blended with the written and spoken word."

As the lights came up with the D-Day landing successful, a military chaplain was seen doing his painful duty of ministering to the dead and wounded. A voice-over recounted how the young man who had been seen handing his letter to the chaplain on the way to France is now among the dead: "He must have thought he was going to make it" the voice-over continues. During the scene, the massed choir sang a medley of songs from the early 1940s—"Lily Marlene," "White Cliffs of Dover," "We'll Meet Again," and "There'll Always Be An England." In the intermission, Don Tremaine, master of ceremonies, asked any present who had served in the uniform of their country to stand and be recognized. Since that tattoo, it has become a tradition to ask those who have served to stand at every performance.

For the commemoration of the end of World War Two in 1945, the focus was not only on remembrance and sacrifice, but on reconciliation and creating bonds of friendship within a new world order, sym-

The Imps Motorcycle Display Team from the United Kingdom

The Canadian Forces Tattoo Staff

A sense of humour may not be essential, but it certainly helps.

Commander Pat Charlton never expected to find himself commanding the Canadian Forces component of The Nova Scotia International Tattoo, but that is exactly what happened...with a little help:

Major Bob Burns was the military protocol officer, Sergeant Bill Lloyd was in charge of ground transport, and Chief Petty Officer Percy Rasmussen was the coxswain. Lieutenant Commander Jack Sparrow was the tattoo staff officer, Petty Officer Sheila Baker handled finance and Petty Officer John Lothian coordinated accommodation and meals. Peter Beech dealt with safety and Secretary Connie Matheson knew everything there was to know about the Canadian Forces and the tattoo.

To those who had served with the Army in some far corner of the world, dealing with the concerns of the tattoo production staff posed quite a challenge. Suddenly they needed to know terms like upstage, downstage, and suddenly they found themselves working with theatrical professionals.

Commander Charlton and his staff would be the first to admit that being part of the team that puts the show together every year is a rewarding experience, and that working in the crazy world of show business takes some adjustment. They didn't take long to conclude that a sense of humour is an advantage when working in this other world. Or, as an old sailor commented as he watched a soldier putting on a wig, "If you can't take a joke, you probably should never have joined up in the first place."

bolized by the fiftieth anniversary of the United Nations. On stage, reconciliation was played out on the Metro Centre floor as a German and a Canadian, both World War Two veterans, along with a German sergeant and a Canadian sergeant, both of whom had served with the United Nations, stood side by side. They declared their friendship and the massed Canadian bands, a German band, and the Tattoo Choir performed Beethoven's "Ode to Joy," alternating verses in English and German. Oberstleutnant Bernd Zivny, Director of Music of the Luftwaffenmusikkorps 4, conducted; he had formerly served in the East German Armed Forces.

Jim Lotz provided historical sketches—"The End of the War in Europe," "In the Air," "At Sea," and "The War with Japan Ends"—in the programme. This programme's design excelled any before it by superimposing type over visuals, a new effect. Nowhere was this more true than in that two-page spread from Lotz's piece, "The End of the War in Europe," which included text superimposed over Alex Colville's "Infantry, Near Nijmegan, Holland," probably the most widely reproduced Canadian painting of World War Two.

To commemorate the service of over one million Canadians, 1995 tattoo poster designer Dave Leonard chose the White Ensign of the Royal Canadian Navy, the Red Ensign for the Canadian Army, and the flag used by the Royal Canadian Air Force, with its maple leaf centred roundel on a blue background. He placed the United Nations logo in the centre of the lower border to signify Canada's peacekeeping role. In previous posters, Leonard had incorporated objects closely associated with the tattoo's public image, such as drums and musical instruments. In the 1995 three-flag poster, the imagery embodied Canada's national pride in its Armed Forces in war and peace. It was a moving and uplifting piece of art work. Leonard's painting was donated to Maritime Command and today hangs in the Department of Defence Building in Ottawa.

A scene from
Again," 1995

In successive years, themes that commemorated our nation's military forces were chosen. For the 1996 tattoo, the main theme was the story of the Canadian Militia, from the beginnings of French settlement through two world wars and to the present peacekeeping era. Two new overseas performing groups to join the tattoo were the Hamburg Police Dog Team and the Lochiel Champion Drill Team. From Ottawa came The Band of the Ceremonial Guard, which performed during the summer months on Parliament Hill for the Changing of the Guard ceremony. The 1997 tattoo juxtaposed the two most pivotal events in the rise of Canada to true nationhood and as a middle power. When the Canadian Corps captured Vimy Ridge in April 1917, Canadians on the battlefield and at home experienced what Lieutenant Greg Clark has called our "first full sense of nationhood." A twenty-year-old

Opposite:
extras portray
June 5, 1944,
before D-Day
1994.

Canadian officer, Lieutenant Eedson Burns was among those who took Vimy Ridge; thirty-nine years later, in 1956, he became commander of the first United Nations Emergency Force (UNEF), which had been deployed on the Suez Canal to keep the peace. For the 1998 theme "The Mounties Go to War," Jim Lotz traced the story of RCMP involvement in Canada's wars from the force's creation in 1873 on the North West frontier, through the South African War, two world wars, and peacekeeping in Croatia. Performing in that tattoo were the Royal Canadian Mounted Police Pipes and Drums and Police Dog Display Team. Measha Gosman and Joe Donahue, both from New Brunswick, and Nova Scotia's Jason Davis appeared as featured vocal soloists in 1998. Gosman would appear again in 2000, this time under her married name, Measha Bruggergosman. Following her performance in the 1998 tattoo, Bruggergosman went on to be featured with Symphony Nova Scotia and is now well on her way to international recognition as a classical vocalist.

"...the imagery embodied Canada's national pride in its Armed Forces in war and peace."

In 1999, Halifax celebrated its 250th anniversary of Edward Cornwallis' arrival with 2,500 settlers, into what was then called Chebucto Harbour on June 21, 1749. For the 1999 tattoo, there could not have been another more historically appropriate theme than Halifax as "Warden of the North." Rudyard Kipling had given the city that name when he penned those timeless words which have ever since, in war and peace, been so evocative in the history of Halifax:

Into the mist my guardian prows put forth,
Behind the mist my virgin ramparts lie,
The Warden of the Honour of the North,
Sleepless and veiled am I!

For the first production in the new century, the tattoo chose as a theme "A Century of Service: A Tribute to Canada's Armed Forces." To mark the event, the tattoo published *A Century of Service: Canada's Armed Forces from the Boer War to East Timor* by Jim Lotz. In her foreword, Her Excellency the Right Honourable Adrienne Clarkson, Governor General of Canada and Commander-in-Chief of the Canadian Forces, wrote that:

Canada's history of military achievement rings with names that contain worlds of meaning and emotion—Ypres, Vimy Ridge, Dieppe, the beaches of Normandy, and Korea. In these places, there were acts of bravery and heroism that are etched into our collective memory. These places are milestones in the Canadian journey, where soldiers stood in defence of our values and earned our thanks and admiration.

Among the new performers for tattoo 2000 were the Celtic Isle Dance Company from Ireland, Band of the Royal Belgian Air Force, Band of the Mounted Arms from the

The Dalhousie Medical Research Foundation

In 1979 the first tattoo was presented and the Dalhousie Medical Research Foundation (DMRF) was established. From that point on, a unique relationship between the organizations developed.

Bill Sobey, foundation chairman, and Dr. Peter Gordon, executive director, saw the opportunity for the tattoo and DMRF to work together. With the encouragement of Dr. Donald Thatcher, Head of Dalhousie University Medical School, and with the support of Graham Dennis of the Halifax Chronicle Herald and Clary Flemming of Clary Flemming and Associates, Dr. Gordon approached the tattoo for permission to do an audio recording of the 1981 production. The first of a series of audio and video recordings grew from this modest request.

As the years went by and the DMRF became involved in other areas of tattoo-related merchandising, substantial revenue was raised for medical research. In 1984, Dr. Gordon was appointed honourary tattoo physician. In 1995, when The Nova Scotia International Tattoo Society was formed with the mandate to reach self-sufficiency, the foundation generously handed tattoo merchandising over to the tattoo society.

Over the past quarter century, The Nova Scotia International Tattoo has become one of the world's leading tattoo productions and a major tourist attraction. At the same time, DMRF has become one of this country's foremost medical research foundations.

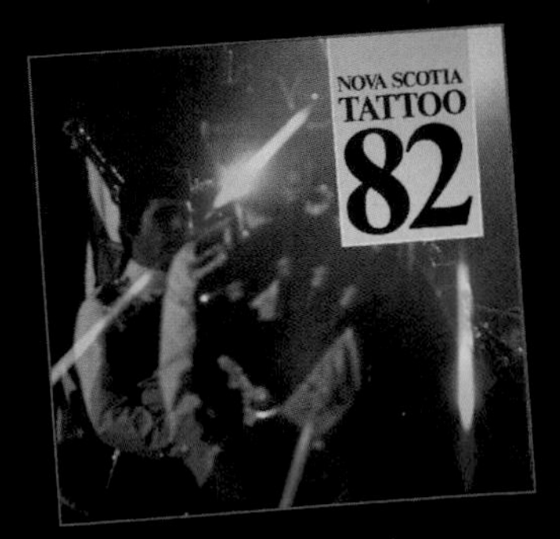

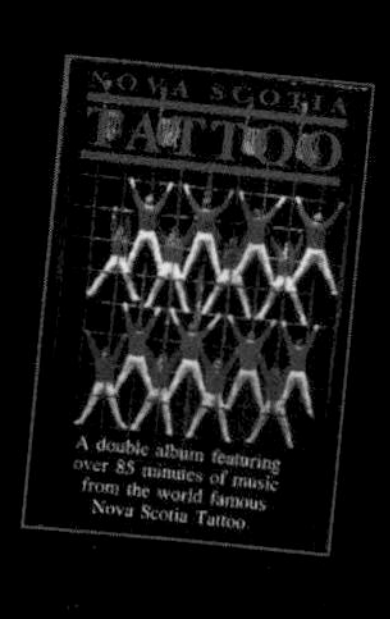

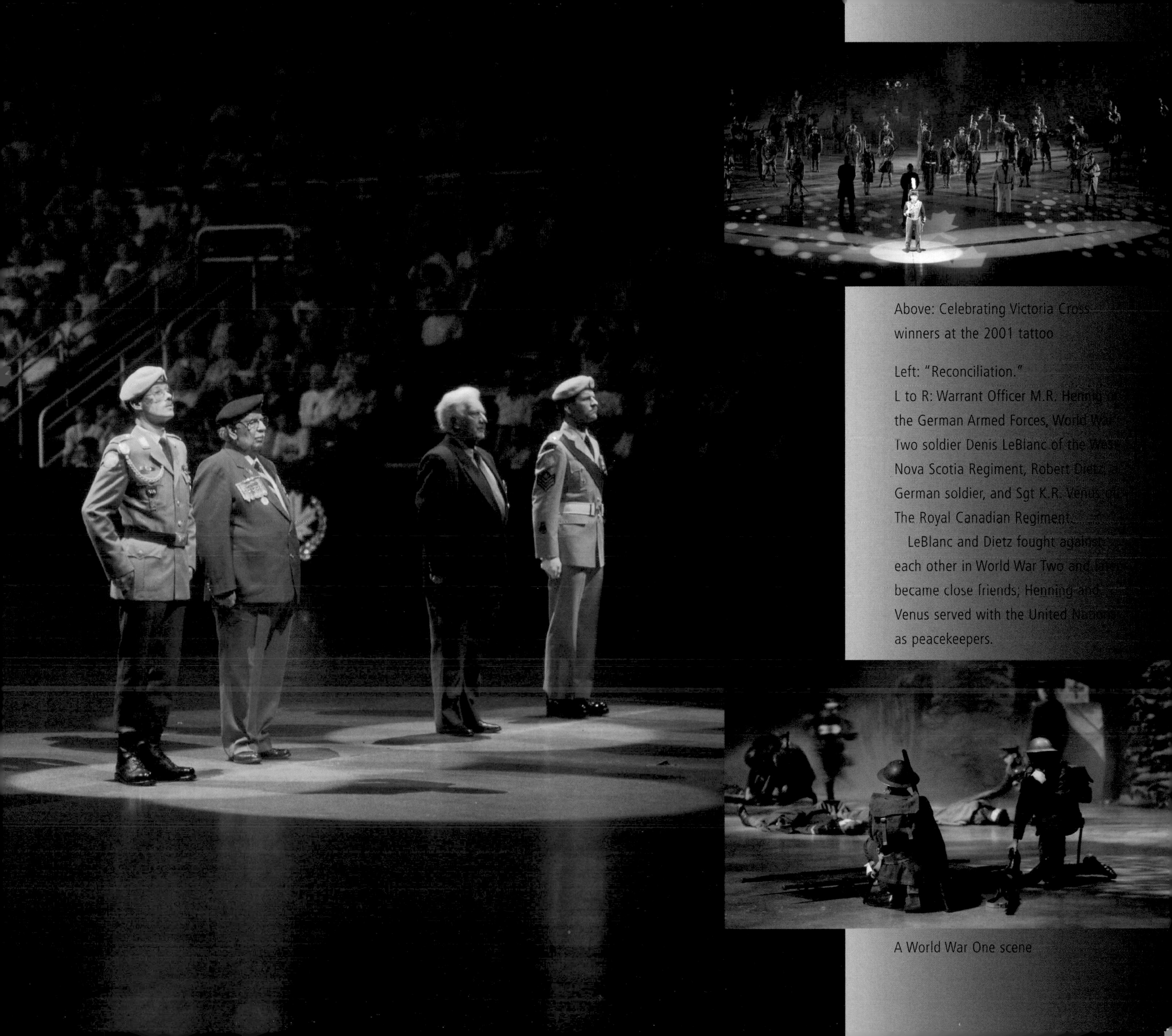

Above: Celebrating Victoria Cross winners at the 2001 tattoo

Left: "Reconciliation."
L to R: Warrant Officer M.R. Henning of the German Armed Forces, World War Two soldier Denis LeBlanc of the West Nova Scotia Regiment, Robert Dietz, a German soldier, and Sgt K.R. Venus of The Royal Canadian Regiment.

LeBlanc and Dietz fought against each other in World War Two and later became close friends; Henning and Venus served with the United Nations as peacekeepers.

A World War One scene

Netherlands, International Taekwondo Mission Display Team from Korea, and, from Edmonton, the Lord Strathcona's Horse Ceremonial Mounted Troop, whose horses had to wear special socks to prevent them from slipping on the Metro Centre floor. Two numbers in the 2000 tattoo were created especially for children—Tales of Mother Goose and Toy Soldiers on Parade. Both the Imps Motorcycle Display Team and the Paris Police Gymnastic Team had returned to the delight of young and old.

Canada's last living Victoria Cross (VC) winner, Ernest Alvia Smith, was the guest of honour for the 2001 tattoo. Private Ernest "Smoky" Smith was serving with the Seaforth Highlanders of Canada during the Italian Campaign, when the battalion was ordered to establish a bridgehead across the Savio River on the night of October 21 and 22, 1944. Although a bridgehead was successfully made, the Germans launched a fierce counterattack. In its repulse, Private Smith, in the words of the citation published in the London Gazette, December 20, 1944,...by the dogged determination, outstanding devotion to duty and superb gallantry of this private soldier, his comrades were so inspired that the bridgehead was held firm against all enemy attacks, pending the arrival of tanks and anti-tank guns some hours later.

Queen Victoria instituted the award in 1856 for officers and men who showed great gallantry during the Crimean War (1854-56). The queen herself suggested the cross, a symbol of sacrifice, for the VC's design. For the 2001 programme, Jim Lotz prepared "For Valour: Canadian Winners of the Victoria Cross," a written and visual account of Canada's VCs, of whom there have been ninety-four. The Victoria Cross continues as Canada's highest decoration to be "awarded for the most conspicuous bravery, a daring or pre-eminent act of valour or self-sacrifice or extreme devotion to duty, in the presence of the enemy." On the medal's obverse side is a lion guardant standing upon the royal crown, and below the crown, a scroll bearing in Latin the inscription "Pro Valore," and on the reverse, the date of the act for which the decoration is bestowed is engraved in a raised circle.

> "...horses had to wear special socks to prevent them from slipping on the Metro Centre floor."

Tattoo 2001 saw three performing groups from Switzerland and another three from Britain. The Gymnastic Club of Mels, Switzerland, practised a form of competitive gymnastics never before seen at tattoos. Its gymnasts, supported by music, performed exercises, displaying a high

degree of synchronization, interpretation of selected music, and technical quality. A totally different group of gymnasts was the D'Holmikers, also from Mels, who presented a version of "Snow White and the Seven Dwarfs." A group of drummers from Basel, "The Top Secret Flying Drumsticks," created an exciting fusion of percussion sets, drumstick juggling and comedy. The "Brigade de Sapeurs-Pompiers de Paris," an extraordinary fifty-man team of gymnasts, all professional Paris firefighters, first appeared at the 1996 Tattoo, and returned in 2001—the Gymnasts' Tattoo.

From Scotland came the Band of the 51st Highland Brigade of the Territorial Army, stationed at Perth, and the Edinburgh Tattoo Ceilidh Dancers. Made up of forty elite dancers, the Ceilidh Dancers gave a spirited performance of intricate jigs and reels—Highland dancing with a twist. From the other end of Britain came Cornwall's St. Keverne Village Youth Band, Champion Youth Brass Band of Great Britain in 1998 and 2000. Also making their first appearances were the Traditional Dancers from the Korean Institute of Missionary Arts and the City of Invercargill Caledonian Pipe Band from New Zealand. Vocal soloists included Allison Bent and Alan Manchester, both of whom had previously performed with the tattoo, and Nicholas Miller, who appeared for the first time in 2001.

Opposite: International
Taekwondo Mission
Team from Korea

New Brunswick's
acclaimed vocalist
Measha Bruggergosman

World War Two Victoria Cross
Ernest Alvia "Smokey" Smith
Maritime Forces Atlantic Tattoo
Logistics Co-ordinator Petty
1st Class John Lothian

The Tattoo Festival

More of the best

The idea probably started when someone suggested that other events at tattoo time would give the thousands of tattoo visitors to Nova Scotia something more to do. The tattoo staff set up a series of concerts and displays, drawing from the enormous talent featured every night during the ten days the tattoo was in town. Staged in downtown Halifax and in the suburbs, these noontime events gave tattoo performers an opportunity beyond the six minutes or so they were given to perform in the show. For want of a better name, the event was called The Tattoo Festival.

Sobeys, the tattoo's leading corporate sponsor, provided some of the festival venues, initially in parking lots at their stores. In 2002, Sobeys took over the Grand Parade and expanded the festival presentations in the centre of Halifax. Other venues in the downtown core were also used, including Historic Properties, Sackville Landing, and the Public Gardens, where hundreds gather every noontime during the summer months.

A small parade on July 1 a few years ago grew to become what is now a centrepiece event for Canada Day. Thousands gather along Spring Garden Road to watch hundreds of tattoo performers take part in the annual parade to help celebrate Canada's birthday. Also, tattoo bands journey to Westville, Lunenburg, and other small communities around the province as part of the tattoo's outreach program.

It may not be a full-blown festival in conventional terms, but it is a pretty good substitute, one that has managed to entertain thousands of Nova Scotians and visitors to the province every summer.

Sea cadets at Sackville Landing in Halifax

Halifax mayor Ron Wallace inspecting
"The Old 18," The Royal Military College of Canada

Sweden's Malmoe Girls Rhythmic Gymnastics Team
on the Grand Parade in 1989

Norm and Fred
Pipes and Drums Duo

In a word association test, nine times out of ten the response to "the tattoo pipes and drums" would be "Norm and Fred."

Norm MacKenzie (sometimes known as Stormin' Norman) became a drum major at age sixteen in his native Perth, Scotland. He has been the tattoo drum major for well over a decade. His focus, which is natural given the fact he is a Scot, is the tattoo pipes and drums, which he organizes each year along with Fred Alderman, the tattoo pipe major. After serving as assistant pipe major for eight years, Alderman became the tattoo pipe major in 1998, and he has never looked back. A former piper with the Canadian Guards and on his retirement from the military, he was the Canadian Forces pipe major and was put in charge of the Canadian Forces School of Music's pipes and drums component.

Very few on the tattoo staff work together more closely than Norm and Fred. Outwitting them as a team is a challenge other members of the staff face every year. As one staff member noted, "Trying to keep up with the two of them is more than most people can manage, but the real problem is going to be the day they add a third member to the team."

Left: Norm MacKenzie
Right: Fred Alderman

D'Holmikers Comedy
Gymnastics Team,
Switzerland

Opposite: Brigade de
Sapeurs-Pompiers de Paris

Overleaf:
Dance Ensemble of
the Northern Fleet
of the Russian
Federation

5 Twenty-Five Years & Looking Forward

2000s Highlights

- Staff Continuity and Change
- "Gang of Five"
- Remembering Dieppe
- 140th Anniversary of the Black Watch of Canada
- September 11th Remembered
- Mainstays and Performers from Away
- International Association of Tattoo Organizers
- Looking Forward
- The Tattoo Finale
- Tattoo Partners, Tattoo Sponsors and The Tattoo Society
- The Tattoo Staff

Planning for 2003, the tattoo's jubilee year, began in 2002 alongside tattoo 2002 planning and production. The tattoo organization had expanded, but surprisingly many of the original production and support staffs remained to undertake tattoo 2002. Still with Ian Fraser as producer/director were Robert Doyle in charge of costume and set design, Jack McGuire as the principal director of music, Earl Fralick as arranger, Walter Kemp as choral director, and Don Reekie as assistant director to Ian Fraser. Ann Montague had first come to the tattoo organization in 1981 as a volunteer script assistant. By the late 1980s she had become the production coordinator and, in practice, became chief of staff, responsible for coordinating all of the creative aspects of each production. Her official title is assistant producer. Don Reekie described Ann as the most efficient person he had ever met. For that first tattoo of 1979, Joe Wallin had been asked to bring his Scottish dance group on board. The group consisted of dancers from Cape Breton, Antigonish and the Halifax area, both adults and children. They did a four-minute routine. For the 2001 tattoo, eighty-five dancers performed Wallin's choreography—presenting patterns, shapes, and movements that were equally pleasing from ground level or from above.

Donald Acaster had continued as the tattoo's lighting designer, but received assistance from David Hignell, who in 1993 had accepted the position of associate lighting designer. In 1999 Acaster assumed the position of lighting designer emeritus, and Hignell took over full responsibility for lighting. Acaster died two years later at his home in British Columbia. In his eulogy, Ian Fraser told the story of how for the 1980 tattoo, Acaster's name had inadvertently been left off the programme credits. On the opening night Acaster refused to switch on the lighting. Fraser, in desperation, asked how he could make amends, to which Acaster replied without hesitation "a grandfather clock." All Fraser could do was to ask "oak or mahogany?" Don Acaster smiled and the lights came on.

The tattoo's first pipe major, Donald Carrigan, served as director of the pipes and drums until his untimely death in 1996. Dave Leonard's portrait of Carrigan appeared on the 1997 tattoo poster and programme. At the finish of the tattoo in 2000, Don Tremaine retired. Doug Bell, assistant director and assistant to Don Tremaine, died within hours of the final performance. Bell had

Tattoo performers “rock around the clock” at the 1989 tattoo

Ann Montague
The "chief of staff"

A good chief of staff must have an eye for detail, be experienced, hard working, organized, smart, loyal, imaginative, tough when required and diplomatic when the situation calls for it.

Ann Montague, the tattoo assistant producer, meets those criteria and then some.

No one knows more about the show, no one has a greater sense of what makes it work, no one else can answer any question about what went on in the past with more accuracy. And no one has a better knowledge of what buttons to push when the going gets tough.

But it didn't happen overnight. A former manager for Targe Productions in 1980 when the company remounted *Meet The Navy*, the World War Two musical, Ann moved on to an executive position in a communications company and from there to tattoo script assistant, production coordinator (with the duties of sponsorship and marketing coordinator thrown in), and now assistant producer.

One of the members of the original "Gang of Five" that puts the show together, she plays a key role in the creative side of the tattoo. When that is done, she has to pull it all together and make it work.

The amazing thing is she does it with great efficiency, style, accuracy, imagination and good humour.

And like a perfect chief of staff, when the bands march off the floor the last night of the tattoo, she is well into planning next year's show.

been with the tattoo since 1981. George Jordan, a well-known CBC radio personality in his own right, took over as tattoo host.

In the planning of each tattoo, the key production staff, known waggishly as the "Gang of Five," forms the first planning level, which selects the acts and generally organizes the show. By 2002, this team consisted of Ian Fraser, Don Reekie, Ann Montague, CWO Tom Peet (drum major of the Band of the Ceremonial Guard in Ottawa and also a tattoo assistant director), and Production Coordinator Jim Forde. Once the first level of planning is complete, the next key group is added to the process; today that group consists of Jack McGuire, Walter Kemp, Tattoo Drum Major Norm MacKenzie, Bob Doyle, David Hignell, Tattoo Pipe Major Fred Alderman, and Joe Wallin. The basic plan is expanded by them to include all music and dancing parts. Most of the primary planning takes place during a week-long production meeting each year in early November.

In addition, there is an operations committee, chaired by the producer/director, including the tattoo commanding officer and representatives from the production staff and the Canadian Forces. This joint committee has the responsibility for the administration and management of all those participating in the tattoo. It meets every six weeks.

Tattoo 2002 proved to be a triumph of soul-stirring and melodious music, flowing and seamless movement, military precision, a kaleidoscope of vivid colour and dramatic presentations. Over nine days some fifty-six thousand people watched and applauded the two-thousand performers from Canada, Norway, Estonia, Germany, the Netherlands, and Japan. Woven into the two acts were a number of commemorative pieces—of the fatal Dieppe Raid in 1942, Her Majesty Queen Elizabeth II's Golden Jubilee celebrations, the one-hundred and fortieth anniversary of the Black Watch (Royal Highland Regiment) of Canada, and the September 11 terrorist attack on the World Trade Centre in New York.

On August 19, 1942, Canada suffered its worst military defeat on the beaches of Dieppe, in a disastrous frontal assault on the French holiday town. Of the roughly 5,000 Canadians who landed, 906 died and another 1,946 became prisoners of war. Whatever lessons were learned in the D-Day Normandy landings, Dieppe continued to haunt Canadians. Neither Jim Lotz's programme piece "Operation Jubilee: Dieppe, 1942," nor the starkly titled scene "Dieppe," attempted to portray it as anything other than a defeat marked by poor planning and bungling, in which the Canadian soldier fought heroically, but to no avail. That three Victoria Crosses were won at Dieppe remains witness to the courage and leadership displayed on that day.

For the "march on," the bands played such stirring reminders of the Queen's Jubilee as "Soldiers of the Queen" and "Here's A Health Unto Her Majesty." In the second act, a scene entitled "Long May She Reign" brought forth Sir Edward Elgar's rousing "Pomp and Circumstance March No. 4."

The year 2002 was the one hundred and fortieth anniversary of the Black Watch regiment's founding. To mark the occasion, the regiment's pipes and drums performed in the tattoo, playing such well-known regimental tunes as "The Red Hackle" and "Wa Sa the 42nd," concluding with "Queen Elizabeth The Queen Mother." Also performing for the first time was the recently formed Nova Scotia International Tattoo/Black Watch Association Pipes and Drums. A call in the autumn of 2001 for volunteers from around the Maritime provinces to become members of a tattoo pipes and drums met with an enthusiastic response, resulting in the selection of thirty-four pipers and drummers. The new band made its first appearance in the 2002 tattoo, dressed in the Black Watch tartan.

In 2002, Stephen Pedersen began his annual *Chronicle-Herald* tattoo review with the words:

The 2002 Nova Scotia International Tattoo achieved perhaps the most emotional moment in its 24-year history at the opening show Saturday night by the simple and significant display of a giant American flag.

A group of tattoo gymnasts entered the south end of the Metro Centre arena holding the brilliantly lit stars and stripes high over their heads at the climax of the first act finale, a tribute to September 11, while Norwegian Kjersti Wiik's soprano voice soared to the rafters with America The Beautiful, to the sonorous accompaniment of full massed bands and choir.

The gymnasts came together with the flag folded between them and when they opened it up again a Canadian flag appeared along side the American. The crowd rose to their feet with a roar, while thousands of hands wiped away tears that rose unbidden to their eyes. The simplicity and sincerity of the gesture erased the borders between countries in a wave of common human feeling.

In his sixth tattoo appearance as a featured vocal soloist, Joe Donahue from Saint John, New Brunswick, sang the memorable "I'll Walk With God" during the September 11 scene. As well, the Dutch Show and Marching Band, Door Vriendschap Sterk, made its first appearance at the tattoo. This band and the Copenhagen Police Band, which had first performed in 1990, were the only foreign civilian bands to perform at tattoos in its near quarter-century history. The Dutch band put on a fast-paced performance, displaying the intricate footwork that made them famous throughout Europe.

Another tattoo first came in 2002 when two Canadian teams from 2nd Battalion The Royal Canadian Regiment and 36 Canadian Brigade Group competed in the obstacle race against a

Poster commemorating The Black Watch (RHR) of Canada and its removal from the Order of Battle in July 1970

From the Black Watch to the Tattoo
From one family to the next

The relationship among members of a Regiment is like a family that supports each other.

Ian Fraser, who had served in the Black Watch (Royal Highland Regiment) of Canada, called on many who had served with him to join the tattoo team over the years.

Dave Ells was a tattoo commanding officer, George Tibbetts was the first tattoo assistant producer, Charlie Campbell, the first sergeant major and he was followed by Wayne Tanner and Nash Harb. Don Reekie became the assistant director, Frank Grant was the first backstage coordinator and Bob Burchill and Harry Philpitt followed him.

Don Carrigan and Bill Gilmour were tattoo pipe majors, John Strong and Peter Goldie, support coordinators and John MacNeil was the tattoo special projects coordinator. They were all members of this very famous regiment and they all served together in Canada's Black Watch at one time or another.

Sometimes called the "Black Watch Mafia" this remarkable team has worked closely together over the years and in the traditional spirit of regimental friendship and loyalty, helped in no small measure to bring The Nova Scotia International Tattoo to where it is today.

That unique relationship continues—the most recent addition being Brian Cuthbertson, who served with the Black Watch and authored this book.

The Army

In the Army officers' mess in Royal Artillery Park in Halifax there is a large oak plaque displaying the names of Army commanders in Nova Scotia, including Lord Cornwallis in 1749. Given the very long association between the army and the province of Nova Scotia, it is more than appropriate that it be a key player in the annual tattoo.

Coordinated by the staff of the army's Atlantic Area, with performers drawn from the Atlantic region, Army participation has included bands drawn from reserve musicians in the four Atlantic provinces, an annual obstacle race, pipes and drums, drill teams, and unarmed combat display. Notably, the Second Battalion, The Royal Canadian Regiment, from Gagetown, New Brunswick, reduced the traditional "trooping of the colour" to twelve minutes to the delight of sixty-thousand spectators over the run of the show.

But Army participation has not been limited to Atlantic Canada. A component of the Ceremonial Guard Band from Ottawa that participates in the Mounting of the Guard every day on Parliament Hill during the summer is also a feature of the tattoo. Over the years, other Army performers—including bands, pipers, display teams and even a troop of horses from the musical ride of the Lord Strathcona Horse in Edmonton—have come from virtually every province.

The annual obstacle race has grown from a simple event in 1979 into a major Army competition. That early obstacle race has been greatly expanded, and made much more difficult; it now features the reserves against the regular force in an annual competition that is completed in less than two minutes. It's worth the price of admission just to see these teams face off in the bone-jarring race. Lord Cornwallis certainly would have enjoyed it.

Canadian Forces electrical/mechanical engineers of the Jeep display team, 33 Service Battalion, Halifax

Below: Soldiers' Race teams on the "A" frame

team from another nation—Norway, His Majesty The King's Guard. Previously, the competing teams had always been from Canada. The Norwegians competed in a series of physically gruelling challenges to win the title of "best obstacle race team" and the Major Doug Bell CD Trophy but it was the Royal Canadian Regiment team that won the race. In their roles as a band and drill team, however, His Majesty The King's Guard's Band and Drill Team was making their second appearance—with good reason: the drill team claimed to be the leading practitioner of precision drill in the world, with their performances of precisely coordinated, complex, and dangerous manoeuvres with rifles and bayonets.

"...displaying the intricate footwork that had made them famous throughout Europe."

Other groups performing in tattoo 2002 included such favourites as the Berlin Police Motorcycle Team, Gym Wheel Team Taunusstein, and Club Piruett Gymnasts. Two new groups—Japan Training Squadron Band and the Japanese Drum Unit, consisting of members from the Japan Training Squadron—made their first appearances. Also performing was Luftwaffenmusikkorps 3, the band of the German Air Force No. 3–Münster.

At the end of tattoo 2002, the tattoo society announced findings by Dr. Helen Mallete of Mount Saint Vincent University of the annual audience survey, which showed that the 2002 production attracted 22,043 out-of-province visitors with an economic impact of $36.2 million. Furthermore, fifty-four per cent of those visitors reported coming to Nova Scotia especially for the tattoo, or cited it as a major influence on their decision to come. These were the best results in the tattoo's history; an added flip was that attendance had gone up nearly ten per cent from 2001.

With tattoo 2002, the show reached a peak in its evolution; it was administratively difficult to extend performances beyond nine or ten days, which limited attendance to around 56,000. As well, twenty-four scenes was probably a maximum if performances were not to run too long. For the last few years, the total number of performers had been about 2,000; in the case of tattoo 2002 there had been 400 musicians, 150 pipers and drummers, and 100 dancers with hundreds more involved in choirs, gun runs, obstacle races, gymnastic displays, and similar acts. As with previous shows, tattoo 2002 had been built up around a core of local military and civilian musicians, pipers and drummers, choirs, dancers, gymnasts, and militia units, not least of all Army, Navy, and Air force cadets, who anchored the show year after year. Moreover, most volunteered their talents and time.

Tattoo 2002 had performing groups from five countries, as well as six Canadian ones from outside Nova Scotia. For the first tattoo in 1979, which coincided with the Gathering of the Clans, nearly all the acts were from Nova Scotia, with

Above: His Majesty The King's Guard's Band and Drill Team, Norway

Below: Central Band of the Swedish Army

The Gun Run
A tradition re-visited

Back in the mid 1960s the production team of the Canadian Forces tattoo, which toured Canada as part of our centennial, decided that a gun run should be part of the show. The Ottawa team designed four sets of equipment and devised a race that was based on the British gun run concept in the Royal Tournament. But this one was a little different. It was no less difficult, but the entire rig could be erected in a matter of minutes and the race that followed was set in an imaginary dockyard during the War of 1812.

Fast forward now to 1980, the year the Canadian Navy celebrated the seventieth anniversary of the Royal Canadian Navy; as part of that celebration, it was decided that a gun run should be in the 1980 tattoo. But that was easier said than done. For starters, no one knew where to find the equipment, and without the equipment that was built in the naval dockyards on both coasts, the race could not be mounted. The task of searching for this much-needed equipment fell to Chief Petty Officer Ray Lawrence, who scoured the country, and came up with all of the bits and pieces. He reassembled the equipment from a number of sources, including a warehouse in Mount Uniacke, Nova Scotia.

The first gun run race since 1967 involved naval reservists, including a group of young officer trainees, some of whom are now senior naval officers and others who have gone on to civilian professions. The event has continued every year thereafter, featuring the East Coast versus the West Coast in a fierce annual competition that was staged for close to a decade. The gun run was part of the 1985 Canadian Forces tattoo, and, except for a brief interruption in 1991 for the Gulf War, the race continued in the Nova Scotia show.

Unfortunately, by 2000, a shortage of available naval personnel forced the gun run to be withdrawn from the tattoo, although a gun run demonstration was presented by a single team in 2002. The field guns, the barrels of which were built by the Canadian Army Research and Development Establishment, the oak trails and limbers constructed in the wheelwright shop in HMC Dockyard in Halifax, and the aluminum uprights and longitudinals built in Victoria now rest in storage.

Gun wheels crossing the chasm

Top: The gun crew firing before the run back
Bottom: The gun barrel being taken across the chasm, followed by the gun trail

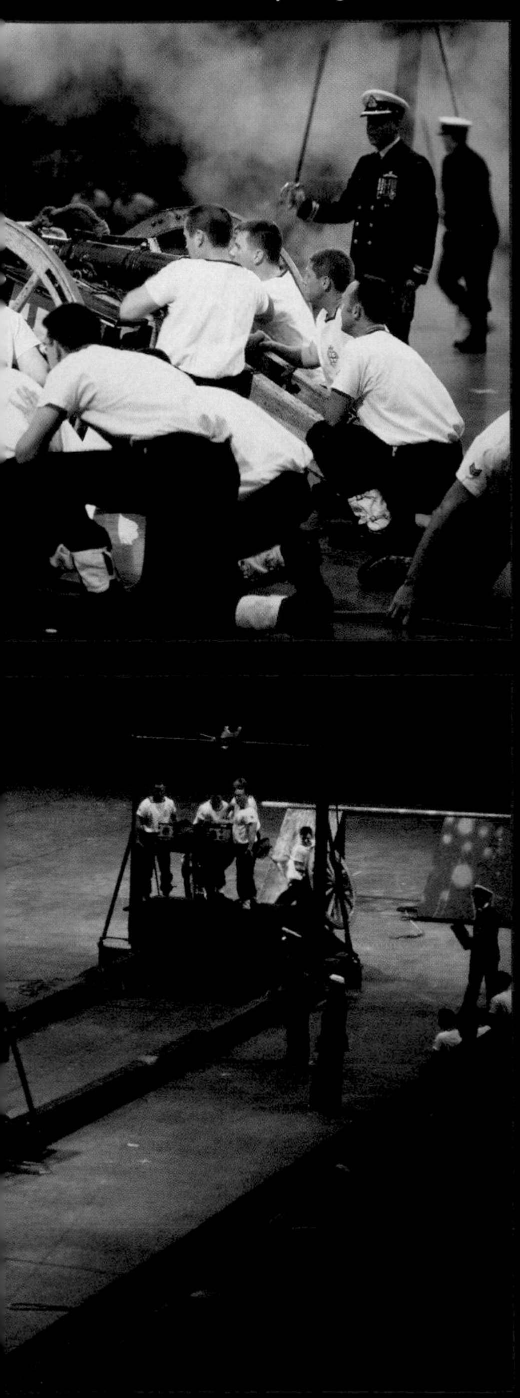

Right: Preparing to lift the gun wheel before crossing the chasm

Vocalists, MU2 Inge Preuss, United States Atlantic Fleet Band, Norfolk, Virginia and Joe Donahue from Saint John, New Brunswick

Scottish groups predominating. Then, in 1980, came the first of many visits by the Quantico Band of the United States Marine Corps. The tattoo had begun the process of attracting foreign performers, though initially this proved difficult, if only because of the high costs that could be involved. A major breakthrough came in 1983 when a German Air Force Band performed. Since that first appearance by Luftwaffenmusikkorps 2, there was not to be a tattoo in which a German military band has not performed.

"Since that first appearance by Luftwaffenmusikkorps 2, there was not to be a tattoo in which a German military band has not performed."

All told, over a quarter century, seventy-eight groups from eighteen countries, excluding Canada, have performed at least once at The Nova Scotia International Tattoo. Most of these were European, with thirty-three from Germany and thirteen from the United Kingdom. As well, the tattoo has been able to attract performers from across Canada. Aside from those in Nova Scotia, twenty-three different Canadian bands and pipes and drums have performed over the years.

Trompetterkorps Bereden Wapens, The Netherlands

In 1997, the first meeting of the International Association of Tattoo Organizers (IATO) took place in Hamburg, Germany. Its main purpose is to meet regularly and assist in the fostering and development of tattoos and similar events worldwide. Founding members were The Nova Scotia International Tattoo, Edinburgh Tattoo, Netherlands National Tattoo, Norwegian Military Tattoo, Swedish Army Tattoo, Hamburg Police Show, Berliner Militärmusikfest, and Virginia International Tattoo.

Since its inception, the Edinburgh Tattoo has placed an emphasis on massed bands and pipes and drums; however, civilian bands and display groups have become more prominent in recent years.

The Netherlands National Tattoo dates back to 1954. Traditionally, it has been almost entirely restricted to Dutch military bands and displays, but more recently international groups have begun making their appearance. For the 2002 tattoo, the pipes and drums of both Vancouver and Calgary police forces along with the Amethyst Scottish Dancers of Nova Scotia and the RCMP participated in the Netherlands tattoo at Breda, the site of the annual outdoor production.

The Norwegian and Virginia tattoos are fairly new events, having begun in the 1990s. They have derived much of their inspiration and format from the Nova Scotian experience. Both are held indoors; as well as numerous military and civilian bands, they attract such groups as Club Piruett from Estonia and the United States Marines Silent Drill Team. Internationally, tattoos have acted to broaden their appeal to a wider audience spectrum, especially tourists, with special emphasis on attracting performing groups from abroad.

In looking forward into the new century, the tattoo has as its principal challenge to remain, in the words of Aubrey Jackman, both "thoroughly modern" and yet continue to have a "life of its own." A life of its own is meant to emphasize that the tattoo concept, traditional or modern, can only retain its uniqueness in the highly competitive entertainment world by never ceasing to be primarily military in the character of its presentation. At the same time, the tattoo is theatre. The Nova Scotia International Tattoo has become the leading exponent of this complementary concept and of the innovative spirit it must foster in order to remain "the greatest show of its kind on earth."

> "...the tattoo has as its principal challenge to remain, in the words of Aubrey Jackman, both thoroughly modern and yet continue to have a life of its own."

Logistics and administration

Turning the lights off at the end of the day

Each November, when the cast for the coming year's show is confirmed, Tattoo Business Manager Barb MacLeod has to develop a logistics and administration plan for hundreds of civilian and foreign performers. Concurrently, deep within Canadian Forces Base Halifax, Lieutenant Commander Jack Sparrow and Connie Matheson have to deal with the administrative details for Canadian Forces performers.

Meetings are held at Dalhousie and Saint Mary's universities, where the performers are accommodated. Nearly a hundred thousand meals have to be arranged; some of these are offered at the universities, others as part of the tattoo meal voucher program, which involves over fifty restaurants around the city. Container shipping and flights from overseas have to be arranged, and the list goes on—finance, currency exchange, medical support, vehicle rental, contracts, cast parties, merchandising...you name it, the logistics and administrative staff does it.

It all comes together in June when Barb and Connie set up the joint military and civilian office in the Metro Centre. They are joined by other members of the administrative staff and the group liaison officers who deal efficiently with many of the day-to-day problems. Things really begin to happen and Murphy's law starts to take over: identity cards are lost...containers are stranded on the high seas...flights are delayed...buses break down...the production staff changes the rehearsal schedule resulting in the need to adjust meal and transportation arrangements in a matter of minutes. It's all in a day's work that starts in the early morning and ends nearly eighteen hours later. As someone once said, it is always the logistics and administrative staff who turn the lights off at the end of the day.

And home again: the German band departing from Halifax International Airport

The Tattoo Finale

All good things must come to an end

Like many ancient military ceremonies, the tattoo finale is steeped in symbolism. Each element in the finale reflects an aspect of the ceremony that took place every night centuries ago after a drummer had marched through the streets, signalling the innkeepers to turn off their taps and warning soldiers to return to camp.

The finale begins with a fanfare, which represents "first post," when sentries were placed around the camp. The march on of the tattoo cast symbolizes the mustering of the soldiers on the parade ground after they returned from the inns and taverns. The evening hymn that follows originated hundreds of years ago in Czarist Russia when the soldiers, who had been conscripted from the deeply religious population, sang a hymn at the end of the day. During the nineteenth century, British regiments adopted the practice. The "last post," when the last guard is posted, is represented at the tattoo by a single bugler, by multiple trumpets or, on occasion, by the music of the full massed bands with their haunting melody interwoven within the evening hymn. Next, a lone piper plays the traditional "Highland Lights Out," a practice common in Highland regiments throughout the Commonwealth. Finally, the national anthems are performed by the massed bands and sung by The Tattoo Choir in the native language of each participating country. The finale is complete when the cast marches out of the arena to the combined bands playing "The Black Bear," a tune of celebration still played by Highland regiments in Canada at the end of a parade.

Tattoo Partners

Tattoo Sponsors

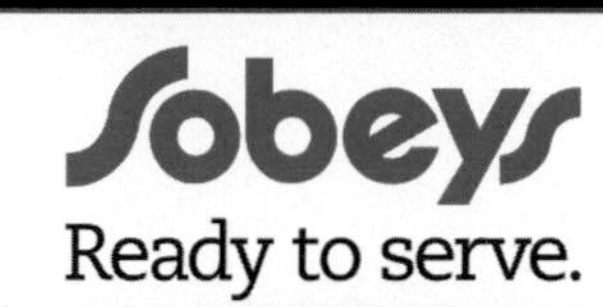

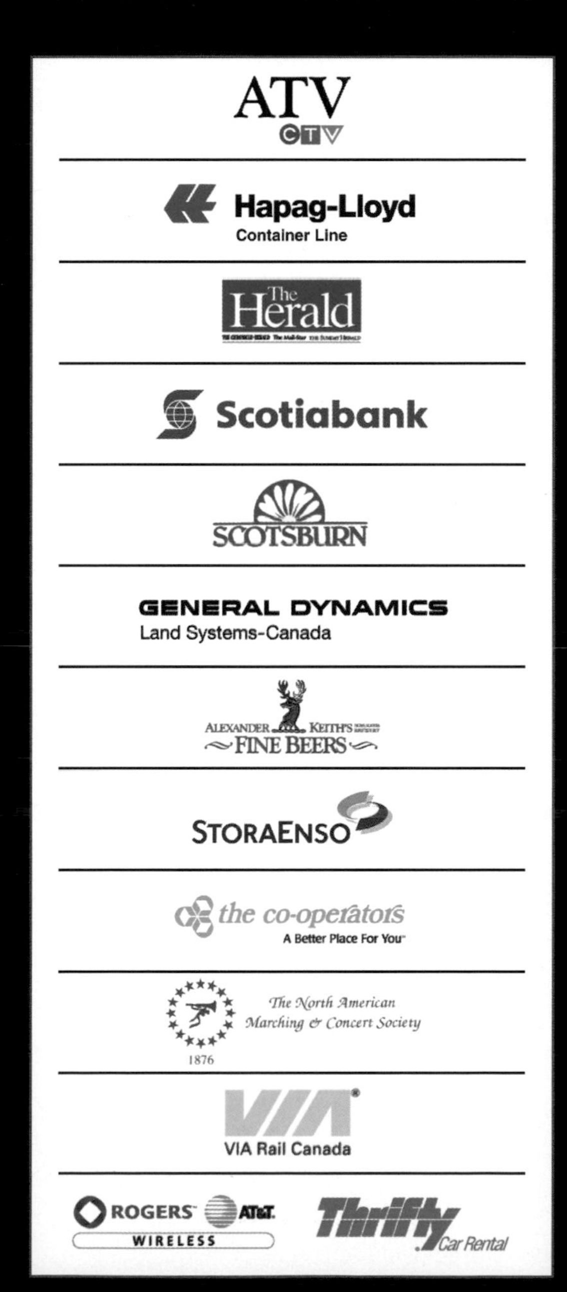

The Tattoo Society

The tattoo is presented by The Nova Scotia International Tattoo Society with a volunteer board drawn from the community at large, including representatives from the Canadian Forces. The not-for-profit society was established in 1995. There were five founding members: Vice Admiral (Ret'd) J.A. Fulton CMM, CD, RCN, a former commander of Maritime Command of the Canadian Forces, George Cooper, Q.C., a Halifax lawyer and former member of parliament, Marilyn Atkinson, formerly director of protocol for the province of Nova Scotia, Jack Keith, a Bank of Nova Scotia vice president, and Ian Fraser, the tattoo producer/director.

The society, now chaired by George W. MacDonald, Q.C., presents the tattoo in partnership with the province of Nova Scotia, the Government of Canada, the Canadian Forces, and the RCMP, along with the Halifax Regional Municipality and the corporate community.

The mission of the tattoo society is "to produce and present a world-class international event that will stimulate Canadian patriotism, educate youth, recognize our country's debt to the Canadian Forces and the Royal Canadian Mounted Police, attract tourists to Nova Scotia, strengthen international relations and enhance the commercial position of tattoo sponsors."

The Tattoo Production Staff

Old Comrades, 1997
From left to right, (back): John MacNeil, Norm MacKenzie, Don Reekie; (middle) Aubrey Jackman, Ann Montague, Ian Fraser, Doug Bell; (front) Pat Laming-Russell, Tom Peet

Older Comrades, 2002
From left to right, (back): John MacNeil, Norm MacKenzie, Don Reekie; (middle) Aubrey Jackman, Ann Montague, Ian Fraser, Jim Forde; (front) Pat Laming-Russell, Tom Peet

The Nova Scotia International Tattoo Production, Backstage and Support Staff 1979 - 2003

Producer/Director
Ian S Fraser *

Production Designers
Fred Allen (Set and Props)
Lin Chapman (Costumes)
Robert Doyle *
Rosemarie Gwilliam (Costumes)
D'Arcy Poultney
Lesley Preston (Set and Props)

Lighting Designers
Donald Acaster
David Hignell *
Brian S. Pincott

Assistant Producers
Ann Montague *
Maj George Tibbetts

Choreographer/Dance Director
Joseph Wallin *

Assistant Directors
Doug Bell
CWO Tom Peet *
Don Reekie *

Principal Director of Music/Arranger
Commander Jack McGuire *

Tattoo Choral Director
Dr. Walter Kemp *

Assistant Principal Director of Music
Capt W.F. Eberts *

Children's Chorus Director
Patricia L. (Guy) Tupper *

Tattoo Drum Major
Norman MacKenzie *

Tattoo Pipe Majors/Pipes and Drums Coordinators
Capt Fred Alderman *
Capt Donald M. Carrigan
CWO A.L. Dewar
CWO W. Gilmour

Drum Majors (Pipes and Drums)
John Cody
Bob Marr

Drum Majors (Military Bands)
Jack Fisher
CPO2 Mike Morley
CWO Tom Peet *

Additional Music Arrangers
Ben Bogisch
Heather Davis
Earl Fralick *
Leo Harinen
Graham Rhodes

Tattoo Fanfare Trumpet Coordinator
CPO Frank Ridgeway *

Tattoo Drumming Coordinators (Pipes and Drums)
Sgt Eugene Heather *
CWO Mike Steele

Tattoo Drumming Coordinators (Military Bands)
CPO2 Bill Brousseau
PO1 Al MacDonald

Massed Band Choreographer/Trainers
PO2 Dennis Collier
Capt F.S. Gannon
PO1 Bob Gaudreau

Lone Pipers
Capt Fred Alderman
Capt Donald Carrigan
General A.J.G.D. de Chastelain
CWO Sandy Dewar
Sergeant Jeff Donnolly
Capt Jermaine Downey
WO Bryan Duguid
WO Ian Ferguson
CWO Bill Gilmour
Jack MacIsaac
Capt Douglas Moulton
PM Bruce Topp

Barbershop Chorus Director
Ian Flemming

Featured Vocal and Instrumental Soloists
PO2 Aldwin Albino
Allison Bent
Janine Blanchard
Steven Booth (Baritone Horn – UK)
Measha Bruggergosman
Willy Cochrane (Dewars Piper)
Brenna Conrad
Diane Covey
Jason Davis
Joe Donahue
Jane Godley
Helen Goodwin-Price
Cpl Rebecca Hiltz LeBlanc
MSgt Hokazono (Euphonium – Japan)
Anita Lathigee
Nancy MacCready
Alan Manchester
Nicholas Miller
Laura Newton
Ruth Phillips
MU2 Inge Preuss, USN (USA)
Gregory Servant
Kathryn Servant
Kjesti Wiik (Norway)

Guest Conductors
Cdr Michael Alverson, USN
LCol J.J.D. Bouchard, CF Supervisor of Music
LCol G.W. Klaassen, CF Supervisor of Music
Cdr G.L. Morrison, CF Supervisor of Music
Oberstleutnant Kurt Ringelmann, Germany,
Oberst Dr. Michael Schramm, Germany
Fregattenkapitän Horst Wenzel, Germany

Associate/Assistant Lighting Designers
James McDowell
Michael Patton *

Production Coordinator
Jim Forde *

Business Managers
Shelley Arsenault
Barbara MacLeod *

Accountant
Brenda Keith

Marketing Coordinators
Brent Feser (Assistant)
Thomas Grotrian (Assistant)
Katherine Handin
Angela Landry
Katherine MacDougall
Robyn McIsaac
Don Shiner
Alexandra Weedon *

Advertising
Bobbie Harrington
Anita Lathigee
Carole McDougall
Scott Tremaine

Backstage Coordinators
Mike Muldoon *
Harry Philpitt

Tattoo Narrators
John Fulton
George W. Jordan *
John Nowlan *
Donald G. Tremaine

Production Manager
MWO Robert Burchell

Assistant Production Manager/Comptroller
Maj Al Brown

Production Assistant
Maj Grant MacLean

Production Consultants
Richard W. Aldhelm-White
Bob Dietz
John Grenville
Pedro Guinard
LCol (Ret'd) W.E.J. Hutchinson
Maj Aubrey Jackman *
Maj Rick Mader
Hamilton McClymont
Wayne Moog

Training Coordinators
CPO1 D.B. Wright

Arena Masters, Assistant Arena Masters and Stage Crew Supervisors
PO2 M. Archambault
PO1 P.A.J. Beauvais
PO2 T.K. Beazley
MS Brian Bennett
MS M Blanchette
WO J. Brackley
MWO Bruce Campbell
MS A. Collier
PO1 Bill Delaney
PO D.R. Deschene
CPO1 Gary Dumas
MS Gordon Dumas
PO2 C.R. Ehler
PO2 M.L. Eng
PO2 J.Y. Gaudet
MS M.J. Hebert
Ms C.E. Hilchey
MS L. Jesso
Michael Johner
STGC Gregory King (USN)
Capt Teresa King
Patricia Kruger
CPO1 Pat Laming-Russell
CPO2 Keith Lawson
PO1 Larry Marshall
PO2 A. Scott McKenzie
Lt (N) J.M.E. Monette
LS W.J. Munro
PO1 M. St-Hilaire
Maj Bill Weagle
PO2 D.K. Wilton
Jake Wttewaall

Stage Crew/Set Construction
CF Fleet School (Halifax)
CF Recruiting, Education and Training System
Her Majesty's Canadian Ships (East Coast)
Maritime Command
Maritime Forces Atlantic
Naval Construction Troop
Naval Reserve Headquarters

European Performers Coordinator
Wilhelm Jaenike *

* incumbent

Technical Directors/Coordinators
PO Jack Drake
Capt Frank Grant
Andre Langevin
David Mardon
Mike Maskell
William Pyke
Colin Richardson *
Dave Stevenson

Set Coordinator
Mary Jane MacLeod *
Phil Sorge

Head Carpenters
Robert M. Backen
Patrick Beauchamp
Robin Creelman (Assistant)
Brian Dawe
Robert A. Elliot
Don Nicholson
John O'Neil (Assistant)
Larry Walker (Assistant)

Audio/Sound Engineers
Russell Brannon
Bill Girdwood
Stéphane Lemay
Guy LeMire
William MacEwan
Al Merson
Alan Strickland
Bruce Thomsen

Assistant Sound Engineers/Technicians
Michael Arnold (Assistant)
Marc Beauchamps (Assistant)
David Brazeau (Assistant)
Christopher Coote (Technician)
Dave Corkum (Coordinator)
Randy Daniels (Technician)
Brian Farr (Assistant)
Bill Girdwood (Assistant)
Ron Gorveatt (Assistant)
Robb Hall (Assistant)
Marc Laliberte (Technician)
Andy Robichaud (Assistant)
Randy Smayda (Assistant)
Frederic St-Onge (Assistant)
Harold Tsistinas (Assistant)

Sound Crew Chiefs
Barry (Scrapper) Stevenson

Lighting
David Bergeron
Robert Brassard
Gary K. Clarke
Tim Crack
Benoit De Carufel (Crew Chief)
Borys Demchynshyn
Marie-Claude Gaboury
Gaétan J. Jalbert
Richard Lafortune
Martin Laurendeau
Jean Francois Mallette
William McDermott
Serge Poupart
Dave Reilly (Crew Chief)
Matt Richman (Crew Chief)
Francois Roupignant
Pierre St-Mars
Michael Still
Valy Tremblay

Riggers
Mike Davis
Dan Grady
Roy Mombourquette
LS Troy Queen
MS J.P. Rondhuis
PO2 B.L. Stanick

Head Electricians
Neil Andrews
Luc Bourget
Jean Francois Canuel
Normand Chasse
Doug Kiddell
Steve O'Connor
Gaetan St-Onge

Costume/Wardrobe Supervisors
Christine Bray
Lin Chapman
Bonnie Deakin
Rosemarie Gwilliam
Jean Kimber
Nancy Leary
Helena Marriot
Marilyn McLaren *

Costume Construction
Dawn Marie Alexander
Abby Anderson
Denise Barrett
Dawn Marie Bayer
Nancy Bell
Gail Beaton
Kathryn Belzer
Carl Bezanson
Stephanie Blackford
Tracy Biggs
Shirley A. Blakley
Tracy Bouchard
Maria Caissie
Marlene Charest
Susan Chase
Betty Chow
Rhonda Coates
Angela Colburne
Brenda Louise Conrad
Stacey Cornelius
Holly Crooks
Shayne Cunningham
Martha Curry
Helene Dahl-Diggins
Mark DeCoste
Laurie Delany
Sara Driscoll
Jacqueline Ann Falle
Monica M. Farrell
Victoria Fenwick
Robin Fisher
Nadine Fletcher
Deborah Fraser
Katie Fraser
Shirley Fuchs
Brad Gould
Rachael Grant
Patty Givogue-Reid
Anna Gudelewicz
Joanna Haney
Josie Harries
Louise Harrington
Julie Horrocks
Sandra Hum
Stephen Hupman
Amé Hutchinson
Catherine Jean Inkpen
Cynthia Jimenez
Minetta Jollimore
Karla Kasdan
Alexandra Kavanagh
Julie Kennedy
Genevieve Killin
Jessy Lacourciere
Clarinda Leach
Dawn LeBlanc
Rhonda LeBlanc
Krista Levy
Sarah Linley
Laura Lee MacKay
Nicole Maquis
Sarah L. Marchant
Meghan Marentette
Iris Y. Mariott
Christina McCaffrey
Carla F. McGrath
Carol L. McNutt
Sandra McNutt
Karen McVey
Catherine Mertens
Alfonsina Metcalf
Jim Michieli
Lynette Muise
Anita O'Toole
Roberta Ann Palmer
Michelle Pelletier
Carmen Perrier
Joan-Kathleen Peterson
Susan Pheiffer
Cara Porter
Brigitte U. Rehwagen
Annie Rempel
Sharon Reynolds
Katherine M. Richmond
Rachael Robatait
Elaine Sanford
Tanya Ann Shaw
Danny Shepard
Beata Slesnski
Tamara Smith
Martha W. Snetsinger
Julia St. Germain
Joan Stewart
Rebekah Streeter
Stella Adenike Tobun
Yesim Tosuner
Patrick Vallèe
Pat Walton
Janice Weatherby
Jay Wells
Meridith Wilson
James Worthen

Tattoo Costume Stores
John McLaren *
MCpl James A. Rogers

Military Historic Uniforms
Marilyn Gurney
Capt G. Melville
Capt M. O'Leary
Barrie Rich

Properties Coordinators/Supervisors
Ken Garant (Radio Controlled Props)
Arie Hakkert (Models)
Sara Hollett * (Pyrotechnics)
Patricia Martinsen *
Jim Morrow (Special Props)
Mary Sadoway
Jennifer Wyatt

Properties Assistants
Sandy Battcock
Cathy Bezanson
Tony Bezanson
Krista Blackwood
Allen Boden
Mark Church
Denise Dolliver
Dorothy Edwards
Lavina Fallows
Nadine Fletcher
Sara Howlett
Jennifer Hunt
Heather Jamieson
Ruth Leggett
Lois Loignon
OS Dwayne Mackie
Vickie Marston
Jane Muldoon
Cynthia O'Brien
Zenovia Sadoway
Darlene Shiels
Jessica Squires
Thelma Phillips
Dan St. Pierre
Peter West

Scene Artists/Painters
John Allen
Hal B. Forbes
Pamela Langille
Richard Marion
Anne Murphy
Thomas P. Paisley
Gary H. Tefler
Lorinda C. Thomas
Wendy Trethewey
Dixie White

Tattoo Logo
Paul Brunelle

Public Affairs and Media Relations
Kathleen Beaton
Katharine Berrington
Pamela Boutilier
Michelle Boylan
Margaret Brill
Capt Ross Brown
LCdr Len Canfield
LCdr Glen Chamberlain
Deborah Chatterton
Anne Marie Coolen
Suzanne Copan
Colin Craig
Maj Tim Dunne
Helene Gauthier
Elizabeth Hagen (Assistant)
Capt John Helle
Nicole Hubbard (Assistant)
Michelle Irwin
Joanne M. Kerrigan
Lt A. B. MacPherson
SLt Peter Magwood
Menna Riley *
Paula Romanow
SLt Penne Ryall
Lt (N) Sue Stefko
Amy Thurlow
Carolyn Townsend
James Wentzell
Maj William Whitehead

Administrative Assistants
Iona Allen
Jennifer Noel *

Program Copy and Additional Script Material
Harry Flemming
LCol (Ret'd) Duncan G.L. Fraser
Jane Greening
Sqn Ldr (Ret'd) Glen Hancock
Jim Lotz *
Guy Simser
William Weagle

Tattoo Poster & Program Designers
Arthur Carter, Paragon Design Group
Cuvilier Communications
Gaynor Sarty Graphic Design
LCol (Ret'd) I.A. Kennedy
Pekka Kauppi
Dave Leonard
Theta Marketing Ltd.
Ken Webb Design

Souvenir Program
Margaret Cassidy
Laura Clement
Heather M. Cochrane
Catherine Eyre
Julie Giles
Anne Graham
Cpl L.D. Hamilton
J. Brian Hannington
Cynthia Henry
Marie Hill
Heather Hueston
Steve Jennex
Ramona Lewis
Ellen E. Overy
Terry Power
Cpl V.A. Riley
Karen Seaboyer
Nicole A. McGillivary
James Wentzell

Electronic Media
Clary Flemming and Associates Ltd.

Tattoo Festival Coordinators
Bill Fell
Maj John MacNeil *

Tattoo Volunteer Coordinators
Lynn Blake *
Margaret Brill
David Church
Lynne Church
Marie Crosby *
Theresa Feltmate
Jamie de Havilland
Ann McLean *

Tattoo Extras Coordinators
David Biggs *
Robin Biggs *
Richard Crowe
J.F. MacNeil
Al McKenzie
WO Don Smith
John C. Tupper
Lester Wood
Graham Young

Special Assistants
Vera Armstrong (Adult Choir) *
Barbara Birks (Dancers) *
Rebecca Campbell (Ticket Coordinator)
Paul Creaser (Adult Choir) *
Margie Colwell (Adult Choir)
Caroline Conliff (Gymnastics)
Thies Eisele (Pipes & Drums Parade)
Annette Graham (Gymnastics)
Anne Hayes (Children's Chorus)
Kori Inkpen (Gymnastics)
Carol Jewett (Parties & Receptions)
Paula Johnson (Gymnastics)
Carol Kemp (Adult Choir)
Valda Kemp (Adult Choir) *
Kelly Lovett (Gymnastics)
Elizabeth MacDonald (Dancers)
Kim MacLeod (Dancers) *
Kerry Maybee (Gymnastics)
Erin Maxner (Children's Chorus) *
Erica McBurney (Children's Chorus)
Coleen McJannet (Adult Choir) *
Wendy Mooney (Dancers) *
Anneke Nielsen (TV Liaison)
Cindy Penney (Dancers)
Jessica Roach (Children's Chorus) *
Jill Simonsen (Dancers) *
Capt Germaine M. Snow (Script)
Colin Stephenson (Gymnastics)
Marjorie Suddaby (Adult Choir)
Michael Thibault (Children's Chorus)
Alexander Tilley (Adult Choir)
Jean Tremaine (Music Data Base)
Emma Tupper (Children's Chorus) *
Mary Ann Wallin (Dancers) *
Bernice Williams (Parties & Receptions)

Gymnastics Coordinators
Lynn Pascoe
Catherine Shortt *
Alexandra Weedon *

Jugglers Coordinator/Magician
Joe Baker

General Duties Supervisor – Civilian Volunteers
David Frid

Civilian Stores Supervisor
Lynn Philpitt *

Extra Voices
Walter Borden
Michael Fitzgerald
Chris MacDonald

Tattoo 50/50 Draw
LCdr Al Turner *

Tattoo Lounge Coordinators
John Harrison *
Alec N. Simpson

Audience Survey Designer/Analyst
Dr. Helen Mallette *
Dr. Norman McGuinness

Tattoo Physicians
Dr. Graeme Bethune *
Dr. Peter C. Gordon

Tattoo Chaplain
Reverend Bob Chapman *

Tattoo Veterinarian
Dr. Paul Kendall

Television Production
Citadel Productions Ltd.
Eastlink Community Television *
Global
MITV

Photographers
Julian Beveridge
Bob Brooks
Michael Coghill
Maurice Crosby
Warren Gordon
Bob Gourlay
Cpl Mel Hayward
Cpl Jerry Kean
Pat Keough
Rosemary Keough
Doug Leahy
Ken Matheson
Sgt Ed Mullin
Norman Munroe
David Nichols (Prisma)
Doug O'Neil *
MCpl Pesant
David Stewart
Maj George F. Tibbetts
CF Photographic Unit (Ottawa)
Formation Imaging (MARLANT)
NS Department of Tourism

Trade Centre Limited
Fred R. MacGillivray, President and CEO *

Halifax Metro Centre
Ken Carver, Box Office Manager
Peggy Dooley, Box Office Manager *
Colin Craig, Promotions Manager
Anita Creaser, Promotions Coordinator
Scott Ferguson, General Manager *
Cheryl Fader, Box Office Coordinator *
Doug Hiltz, Pyrotechnics *
Randy Johnson, Event Manager *
Keith D. Lewis, General Manager
David Mills, Electrician *
Pat Murray, Box Office Manager
Linda Poulton, Assist. Box Office Manager *
David C. Stevenson, Operations Manager
Ralph Williams, Event Manager *

Tattoo Commanding Officers
Cdr D.C. Beresford-Green
Capt (N) L.J. Cavan
Cdr Patrick Charlton *
Cdr John A. Creber
Col David B. Ells
Col Bruce Gilchrist
Cdr Barry S. Munro
Capt (N) Arthur L. Vey

Chief Petty Officers/Sergeant Majors
CPO1 Craig B. Calvert
MWO C.A. Campbell
MWO Nash Harb
CPO1 Ray Lawrence
CWO D.G. Lemoine
CPO1 Fred McKee
CPO2 Percy Rasmussen *
MWO B.W. Tanner

Senior Staff Officer
LCdr J.B. Sparrow *

Tattoo Secretary
Connie A. Matheson *

Support Coordinators
Maj K. Bourgeau
Capt G.F. Coady
WO E.A. Dunfield
Capt K. Gingell (Assistant)
Capt Peter Goldie
Lt H.A. Higgins (Assistant)
PO1 John Lothian *
SLt A.B. Patterson
Maj John R. Strong

Administration and Logistics Coordinators
Capt G.F. Coady
LCdr D.S. Chandler
Maj L.G. Del Villano
Lt Kim MacNeil
Maj Willard R. MacNeil
Lt (N) Michelle McNichol
LCol D.R.B. Rogers
Maj J.H. Trethewey
Maj K. Whitehead

Chief Clerks
Cpl D.J. Alberta
CPO1 M.C. Anderson
WO K.J. Bakes
MS S.A. Butler (Assistant)
MWO B.C. Campbell
Sgt O.F. Cleary
CPO2 Stan Gilles
WO Angela Moffatt
PO2 H.M. Oake
Cpl S.L. Weatherton

Finance Coordinators
PO1 Sheila Baker *
MWO Jim Campbell
CPO1 Bill Levack

Protocol Officers
Maj Robert Burns *
Capt J.E. Dunn
LCdr A.J.W. Holmes
Capt S.J. Jenkins
OCdt R.F. Wight

MARLANT Coordinators (Navy)
LCdr Peter Townsend
CPO2 Jack Morgan

LFAA Liaison Staff
LCol D. Nauss
Major C. Flood

LFAA Coordinators (Army)
Capt John F. Mahon
Capt Rob Johnson
Capt W.A. Sweet
Capt John Todd *

MAC (A) Coordinators (Air Force)
Maj Don Feltmate
Capt Chris Muise
Capt D.W.J. Robinson
Capt Chris Semeniuk *

36 Brigade Group Coordinator
Capt Jim Molloy *

36 Brigade Group Warrant Officer
WO D.K. Hannigan *

Maritime Air Component (Atlantic) Warrant Officer
MWO T.E. Bellefontaine *
MWO K.P. Connors

Militia/Reserve Coordinators
Maj Tom Howland

Pit Band Directors of Music
LCdr Gaetan Bouchard * (Stadacona Band)
Capt Don Embree (RCR Band)
Lt (N) Jim Forde (Stadacona Band)
LCdr Peter van der Horden (Stadacona Band)
Lt (N) Ron McCallum (Stadacona Band)
Lt (N) Hugh McCullough (Stadacona Band)
Lt (N) George Morrison (Stadacona Band)
Lt (N) B. Tempelaars (Stadacona Band)

National Band of the Naval Reserve Directors of Music
Lt (N) Francois Ferland *
LCdr Alexandra Kovacs-Ada
Cdr J.F. McGuire

Land Force Atlantic Area Band Directors of Music
Capt Mike Chalmers
Capt William F. Eberts
Capt David Jackson *
Maj Gerry S. Pheby

Ceremonial Guard Band Directors of Music
Capt Scott W. Attridge
Capt Jacques Destrempes
Capt Brian Greenwood *
Capt Ray Murray

Liaison and Special Project Coordinators
LCol Ernie Beno
LCol Bob McLean

Special Events Coordinator
George Borden

Cadet Coordinators
Capt S.L. Cater
Maj P.A. Chatterton
LCdr Ray Halliday
Capt Blair Hawco
Maj E.C. Lantz
SLt E.A. Lindsay
Capt J.E Orr

Orderly Room
WO K.J. Bakes
Cpl D.E. Bazinet
LS D. Holt
LS S.E. Hunter
Sgt K.J. MacDonald
PO2 R.A. Smith

Computer Programmer
LCdr A.D. Gorman
Leonard Landry

Graphic Artist
WO Owen Kingwell

Military Stores
MCpl M.A. Brooks
LS L. Clifford
Capt K.W. Elloway
MWO R.L. Gracie
MCpl Robert Hendsbee
PO2 P. Horne
Cpl S.R. Lafleur
MS Krista L. Langille
GNR Alexandra Lothian
PO2 B.M. Marsh
Cpl J.A. Matheson
MS D.M. Monk
MS W. Oldford
Pte G.J. Walker
MCpl G.F. Walsh
LS W.E. West

Food Service Coordinators
SLt T. Helm
Lt Mario Hubert

Medical Coordinators
WO D.E. Libby *
33 (Halifax) Medical Platoon

Transport Supervisors
MCpl L. Brown
Sgt O.C. Burton
Sgt H.A. Greer
Sgt T.B. Hutchinson
MCpl C.P. Kennedy
Sgt J. Kozeil
Sgt W.L. Lloyd *
Sgt G.E. Sherritt

Security Coordinator
Sgt K.R. Briggs
Sgt J. Devries
Sgt D.E. Galloway
MCpl F. Hallett *
Sgt J.A. Leclerc
PO2 I.R. Rice
Sgt O.L. Richard

Liaison Officers
Lt (N) M.J. Alexander
CPO Serge Becelaere (Belgian Navy)
PO2 Ralph Beckerschoff
SLt A.P. Bedard
LS T.R. Bourgoin
CWO P.J. Buiteman
Lt G. Caladrino, USN
WO J.F. Cameron
SLt A.M. Chang
Capt M.A. Chisholm
Seung Hyuk Choi
Dae-Jin Chun
Lt (N) H.P. Collins
Lt (N) P.M. Egener
CPO Rudy Eneman (Belgian Navy) *
Lt (N) R.D. Espey
Fernando Fernandez
Lt Kimberley Gingell
MS M. Grant
Geon Soon Han
PO2 Susan Hayes
Capt Willard Hinkley
PO1 A.E. Hone
Lt (N) Roman Husiuk
Lt (N) John Hutchinson
Capt Lloyd Jackson
Sgt G.G. Jensen
Lt (N) A.C. Kados
Kyung-Oh Ko
Lt (N) Christian Kowalski
LS S.R. Legault
Judith Lothian *
Poul Mathieson
PO2 Andres C. Mazurimm
Gail Melvin
LCdr P.G. Miller, USN
Capt Gerd Moritz
PO1 E.P. Muehleisen
Capt Terry Otsuji
Dr. Felix Park *
Cst. A. Pattison
Lt (N) (Ret'd) Paul Phillips *
PO1 Bill Uhrig
Elsbeth Reid
Maj F Rhese
Lt (N) K. Riebe
Lt (N) Johannes Sauerteig *
SLt M.J. Schultz
MWO F. Stubbert
Lt (N) S.W.D. Swan
Capt Ward A. Sweet
Lt (N) D. Taylor
LCdr M. Taylor (Russian Ships Visit)

Lt (N) B. Traenor
LS Frank Wanke
Lt (N) M.B. Watson
Lt (N) D.L. Wells
WO H. Wesenberg

Military General Duties Supervisors
LS Wayne Boone
MS A.J. Gaudet *
LS S.J. Locke
Sgt D.J. Meldrum

Hull Technicians/Carpenters
D. Barrett
PO2 J.R.Y. Bouthat
LS Terry Connors
LS C.C. Cummings
LS T.M. Deazley
LS F.C.P. Frenette
AB P.D.V. Gerroir (Assistant)
MCpl J.S. Green
Cpl F.J.P. Hetu
PO1 J. Jackson
PO2 L.M. Keizer
MS E.L. Kellner
MS Lloyd Kerslake
Cpl J.F. Lassard (Assistant)
MS J.E. Mason
PO1 P. Russell
PO1 Trevor Spring
MS B.E. Woods *
Sgt P. Woodward

Safety Officers
Lt (N) D. Anderson
Sgt B. Archambault (Assistant)
Peter Beech
Lt (N) D.B. Collins
CPO2 Denis Descoteaux
SLt P.S. Duke
PO1 P.M. Harrod
PO1 T.R. Johnson
PO1 L. Legaarden
PO1 John Matheson *
Lt (N) Gary Reid
Lt (N) D.W. Rutherford
PO1 J.F. Sheppard
OTMC L.R. Vargas, USN
MS L.R. Waye

Accommodations Supervisors
CPO2 B.J. Amirault
MS J.M.C. Bergeron
PO2 M. Breault
LS G.R. Harris
PO2 W.H. Hutching
LS D.G. MacMullin
LS A.R. McDow
Sgt A.M. Richard
PO1 (Ret'd) A.J. Simpson
LS J.G.D. Villineuve

Military Stores Driver
LS C.D. Broyden

DND Customs Broker
Mike Smith *

RCMP Coordinators
Supt C.A.J. Bungay
Insp J.P. Curly
Insp Keith Sherwood *
Chief Supt W.B. Vye

RCMP Instructors/Trainers
SM Robert Gallup *
Cpl Brian McCarthy
Sgt Garth Patterson
Cpl Bill Price
SSM Debbie Reitenbach *

Many have performed multiple roles in the tattoo since its inception. The majority have been listed in their most recent position.

We pay tribute to all who have played a part in the production of The Nova Scotia International Tattoo over the past twenty-five years. There are literally hundreds of volunteers, backstage workers, musicians, dancers, gymnasts, artists, technicians, production and support staff, both military and civilian, who are unnamed and probably unknown—thank you all!

Special thanks to Capt Ian Briggs, RCA and Charlie Johnson, RHC

Tattoo Performers 1979-2003
1st Battalion, Nova Scotia Highlanders (North)
1st Battalion, Nova Scotia Highlanders Pipes and Drums
2nd Battalion, Nova Scotia Highlanders (Cape Breton)
2nd Battalion, The Royal Canadian Regiment
2nd Battalion, The Royal Canadian Regiment Pipes and Drums
12 (Nova Scotia) Field Squadron Royal Engineers
33 Service Battalion Pipes and Drums, Halifax NS
48th Highlanders of Canada Pipes and Drums
78th Highlanders
78th Highlanders Ross Shire Buffs
84th Regiment of Foot (Royal Highland Emigrants)
428 Tactical Helicopter Squadron Band, St. Hubert QC
Air Command Pipes and Drums
Air Command Precision Drill Team
American All Star Dancers
Atlantic Region Tri-Service Cadet Brass Reed Band
Atlantic Region Tri-Service Cadet Pipes and Drums
Atlantic Swells, Halifax NS
Australian Army Band, Brisbane
Balmoral Girls Pipe Band, Stellarton NS
Band of 1 Canadian Air Division, Winnipeg MB
Band of 51 Highland Brigade, UK
Band of the 1st Airborne Division, Stuttgart Germany
Band of the 1st Mountain Division, Garmisch-Partenkirchen Germany
Band of the 3rd Armoured Division, Lüneburg Germany
Band of the 10th Armoured Division, Ulm Germany
Band of the 12th Armoured Division, Veitscöchheim Germany
Band of Her Majesty's Royal Marines, UK
Band of the Ceremonial Guard, Ottawa ON
Band of the Royal Netherlands Air Force, Netherlands
Bedford Skippers Gymnastics Team
Bermuda Islands Pipe Band
Bermuda Regiment
Blue Hackle Pipe Band, Amherst NS
Blue Thunder (Halifax and Dartmouth Police)
Bluenose Jugglers
Bugle Platoon of the 3rd Battalion The Light Infantry, UK
Bremerhaven Dancers, Germany
Brigade de Sapeurs-Pompiers de Paris, France
Calgary Fiddlers, Calgary AB
Calgary Highlanders, Calgary AB
Calgary Police Service Pipe Band, Calgary AB
Calgary Stampede Show Band, Calgary AB
Canadian Airborne Regiment
Canadian Forces Base Borden Pipes and Drums, Borden ON
Canadian Forces EME Jeep Display Team, Borden ON
Canadian Forces Fleet School (Atlantic)
Canadian Forces Music Detachment Pipes and Drums, Borden ON
Canadian Forces Recruit School, Cornwallis NS
Canadian Forces School of Music
Canadian Forces Vimy Band, Kingston ON
C.B. Hoare Pipe Band, Sydney NS
Ceilidh Pipe Band, New Glasgow NS
Celtic Isle Dance Company, Ireland
Central Band of the Canadian Forces, Ottawa ON
Central Band of the Japan Air Self Defense Force, Japan
Central Band of the Swedish Army, Sweden
City of Invercargill Caledonian Pipe Band, New Zealand
City of Lakes Chorus, Dartmouth NS
Clan MacFarlane Pipe Band, St. Catherine's ON
Club Piruett, Estonia
Cobequid Spartans
Colchester Legion Pipe Band, Colchester NS
Commissioner's Own Ontario Provincial Police Pipes and Drums
Copenhagen Police Band, Denmark
Corps of Drums of the 1st Battalion, The Royal Canadian Regiment
D'Holmikers Comedy Gymnastics Team, Switzerland
Dalhousie Boys Gym Club
Dalhousie Gym Club
Dance Troop "Jeans', Netherlands
Dartmouth Boys Pipes and Drums
Dartmouth Legion Pipe Band, Dartmouth NS
Dartmouth Titans
Delta Police Pipe Band, Delta BC
Dukes of Kent, Kentville NS
Dunvegan Girls Pipe Band, Westville NS
Dutch Show and Marching Band "Door Vriendshap Sterk", Katwijk Netherlands
Edinburgh Tattoo Ceilidh Dancers, UK
Fanfarekorps Koninklijke Landmacht
Flying Danish Superkids, Aarhus Denmark
Flying Grandpas, Hamburg Germany
Flying Saxons, Zwickau Germany
Flying Stevens, Sweden
Fraser Holmes Memorial Ladies Pipe Band
Fredericton Society of St. Andrews Pipe Band, Fredericton NB
German Rock 'n Roll Acrobatic Dancers
Ginásio Clube Português, Lisbon Portugal
Gospel Heirs
Gym Wheel Team Taunusstein, Germany
Gymnastic Club of Mels, Parallel Bar Team, Switzerland
Halifax City Gymnastics Club
Halifax Police Association Pipes and Drums
Halifax Tumblebugs
Hamburg Police Dog Team, Hamburg Germany
Hants East Gym Club
Heeresmusikkorps 4, Regensburg Germany
Heeresmusikkorps 7, Düsseldorf Germany
Heeresmusikkorps 9, Stuttgart Germany
Heeresmusikkorps 100, Münster Germany
Heeresmusikkorps 300, Koblenz Germany
Highland and Scottish Country Dancers
Highland Society of Antigonish Gaelic Choir, Antigonish NS
Highland Village Pipe Band, Iona NS
His Majesty The King's Guard's Band and Drill Team, Oslo Norway
Imps Motorcycle Display Team, London UK
Infantry Section, 2nd Battalion The Royal Canadian Regiment
International Taekwondo Mission Display Team, Republic of Korea
Japan Training Squadron Band
Juergen Baumgarten, Germany
Juliana Bicycle Team, Netherlands
Land Force Atlantic Area Army Band
Light Infantry Corunna Band, UK
Lochiel Champion Drill Team, New Zealand
London Irish Rifles Regimental Association Pipes and Drums, UK
Lord Strathcona's Horse (Royal Canadians) Ceremonial Mounted Troop, Edmonton AB
Lord Strathcona's Horse (Royal Canadians) Pipes and Drums, Edmonton AB
Lothian and Borders Police Pipe Band, Edinburgh UK
Luftwaffenmusikkorps 1, Munich Germany
Luftwaffenmusikkorps 2, Karlsruhe Germany

Luftwaffenmusikkorps 3, Münster Germany
Luftwaffenmusikkorps 4, Berlin, Germany
MacDougall Girls Pipe Band, Glace Bay NS
MacNaughton's Vale of Atholl Junior Pipe Band, UK
Malmoe Girls, Malmoe Sweden
Marinemusikkorps Nordsee, Wilhelmshaven Germany
Marinemusikkorps Ostsee, Kiel Germany
Maritime Forces Atlantic Gun Run Display Team
Maritime Forces Atlantic Naval Display
Men of the Deeps
Metropolitan Toronto Police Pipes and Drums, Toronto ON
Milling Frolic and Step Dancers
Motorcycle Display Team of the Berlin Police Force, Germany
National Band of the Naval Reserve
North Preston Ancestral Community Choir
Nova Scotia Highlanders Combined Pipes and Drums
Nova Scotia International Tattoo/Black Watch Association Pipes and Drums
Nova Scotia Tri-Service Cadet Display Team
Novatones, Truro NS
Old Guard Fife and Drum Corps, Washington DC
Paris Police Gymnastic Team, France
Pipes and Drums of the 2nd Battalion, The Royal Canadian Regiment
Pipes and Drums of the 51st Highland Regiment
Pipes and Drums of the Black Watch (RCR) of Canada
Polska-Lechowia Polish Canadian Folk Dance Company, Toronto ON
Pomorze Polish Dancer Ensemble, Halifax NS
Princess Louise Fusiliers, Halifax NS
Princess Patricia's Canadian Light Infantry Band, Calgary AB
Princess Patricia's Canadian Light Infantry Regimental Drum Line, Calgary AB
Principal Band of the French Foreign Legion, France
Privateersmen, Liverpool NS
Quantico Band of the United States Marine Corps, Quantico Virginia
Queen Victoria School Pipes, Drums and Dancers, UK
Queen's Colour Squadron of The Royal Air Force, Middlesex UK
Queen's Gurkha Engineers Pipes and Drums, UK
Queen's Own Cameron Highlanders Pipes and Drums
United States Army Drill Team, Washington DC
United States Army Herald Trumpets, Washington DC
United States Atlantic Fleet Band, Norfolk Virginia
United States Continental Army Band, Norfolk Virginia
United States Navy Band "Country Current," Washington DC
Rhythm Project, Norfolk Virginia
Royal Artillery Animation Unit
Royal Australian Navy Physical Training Display Team
Royal Band of the Belgian Air Force, Brussels Belgium
Royal Canadian Air Cadet Squadrons, Nova Scotia
Royal Canadian Army Cadet Corps, Nova Scotia
Royal Canadian Artillery Band, Montreal QC
Royal Canadian Mounted Police
Royal Canadian Mounted Police Dog Display Team
Royal Canadian Mounted Police Pipes and Drums
Royal Canadian Regiment Band
Royal Canadian Sea Cadet Corps, Nova Scotia
Russian Cossack State Dance Company
Royal Military College of Canada
Sackville Taisos
Scotia Legion Pipe Band, Halifax NS
Scots College Pipes and Drums, Sydney Australia
Soldier's Obstacle Race
Song and Dance Ensemble of the Northern Fleet of the Russian Federation
Sons of the Sea, Lunenburg NS
South Shore Kippers
Souwesters, Yarmouth NS
Sprigs of Heather Pipe Band, North Sydney NS
Stadacona Band of Maritime Forces Atlantic
St. Keverne Village Youth Brass Band, UK
Tattoo Barbershoppe's Chorus
Tattoo Children's Chorus
Tattoo Choir
Tattoo Dancers
Tattoo Fanfare Trumpets
Tattoo Gymnasts
Tattoo Junior Dancers
Top Secret Flying Drumsticks, Switzerland
Toronto Scottish Regiment Pipes and Drums
Traditional Dancers from the Korean Institute of Missionary Arts, Republic of Korea
Trompetterkorps Bereden Wapens (Band of the Mounted Arms), Netherlands
Truro Flyers
VanGorder Illusionists
West Nova Scotia Regiment, Aldershot NS
Woods Manufacturing Company Brass Band, Stittsville ON
Wylde Thyme Pipes and Drums, Halifax NS
Youth Singers of Calgary, Calgary AB

● The Nova Scotia International Tattoo Society

Board of Directors

LCol, The Honourable Alan R. Abraham
Tina V. Battcock
Col (Ret'd) J.B. Boileau
David J. Bright
Col (Ret'd) John M. Cody
Cmdre (Ret'd) David Cogdon
Capt (N) (Ret'd) B. Elson
Ian S. Fraser
VAdm (Ret'd) James King
Michael Kontak
James M. MacConnell
George W. MacDonald - Chairman
Bill McEwan
Kenneth M. Mounce
John A. Morash
David H. Nurse
Rob G. Sobey
Donald G. Tremaine

Members

VAdm (Ret'd) J. Allan
Adm (Ret'd) J.R. Anderson
Margaret Amour
Marilyn Atkinson
J. Bernard Boudreau
Senator, The Honourable John M. Buchanan
VAdm (Ret'd) P.W. Cairns
The Honourable Donald W. Cameron
George Cooper
BGen (Ret'd) C. Curleigh
RAdm Glenn V. Davidson
Capt (N) (Ret'd) H. Davies
Larry Doane
Brian Flemming
VAdm (Ret'd) J.A. Fulton - Chairman Emeritus
VAdm (Ret'd) G.L. Garnett
VAdm (Ret'd) R.E. George
Col (Ret'd) B.C. Gilchrist
Ruth M. Goldbloom
The Honourable John F. Hamm
Bernie Hum
Jack Keith
VAdm Bruce MacLean
The Honourable Russell MacLellan
VAdm G.R. Maddison
Lois Dyer Mann
Annette Marshall
VAdm (Ret'd) L.G. Mason - Chairman Emeritus
Jack MacIsaac
VAdm D.E. Miller
Julia Sagebien
The Honourable John P. Savage
John R. Sobey
Karl R. Sobey
J. Stuart Sullivan
VAdm (Ret'd) C.M. Thomas
Barbara Watt
VAdm (Ret'd) J. C. Wood
Michele Wood-Tweel

● Premiers – Province of Nova Scotia

John M. Buchanan 1979–1990
Donald W. Cameron 1991–1992
John P. Savage 1993–1997
Russell MacLellan 1998–1999
John F. Hamm 2000–

● Commanders Maritime Command

Vice-Admiral A.L. Collier 1979
Vice-Admiral J. Allan 1980
Vice-Admiral J.A. Fulton 1981–1983
Vice-Admiral J.C. Wood 1984–1987
Vice-Admiral C.M. Thomas 1988–1989
Vice-Admiral R.E. George 1990–1991
Vice-Admiral J.R. Anderson 1992
Vice-Admiral P.W. Cairns 1993–1994
Vice-Admiral L.G. Mason 1995–1996

● Commanders Maritime Forces Atlantic

Rear-Admiral G.L. Garnett 1996
Rear-Admiral G.R. Maddison 1997
Rear-Admiral D.E. Miller 1998–2000
Rear-Admiral Bruce MacLean 2000–2002
Rear-Admiral G.V. Davidson 2002–

● Commanders Land Force Atlantic Area

Major-General R.R. Crabbe 1996–1997
Brigadier-General H.C. Ross 1998
Brigadier-General D.W. Foster 1999
Brigadier-General G.B. Mitchell 2000–2003
Brigadier-General R.R. Romses 2003–

● Commanders Maritime Air Component (Atlantic)

Brigadier-General B.N. Cameron 1996–1997
Colonel J.L. Orr 1998–1999
Colonel M.W. Haché 2000–

● Royal Canadian Mounted Police

Chief Superintendent H.A. Fagan 1979–1980
Chief Superintendent C.J. Reid 1981–1988
Chief Superintendent G.G. Leahy 1989–1990
Asst. Commissioner A.D.F. Burchill 1991–1995
Asst. Commissioner R.F. Falkingham 1996–1997
Asst. Commissioner D.L. Bishop 1998–

● Mayors—City of Halifax and Halifax Regional Municipality

Edmund Morris 1979–1980
Ronald J. Hanson 1980
Ron Wallace 1981–1991
Moira Ducharme 1991–1994
Walter Fitzgerald 1994–2000
Peter Kelly 2001–

● Chairman—The Nova Scotia Tattoo Committee

Vice-Admiral (Ret'd) J.A. Fulton 1986–1987

● Chairman - The Nova Scotia International Tattoo Committee

Vice-Admiral (Ret'd) J.A. Fulton 1988–1994

● Chairmen—The Nova Scotia International Tattoo Society

Vice-Admiral (Ret'd) J.A. Fulton 1995–1998
Vice-Admiral (Ret'd) L.G. Mason 1999–2001
George W. MacDonald, QC 2002–